Through The Seasons

Through the Seasons
with
The Write Gardener

TC Conner

TC Conner
"The Write Gardener"

Illustrations by Donald Conner

Front cover photography: TC Conner, (plants pictured: chrysanthemums, crocus, spruce tree and sunflower).

Illustrations by Donald Conner.
Email - donthesawyer@insightbb.com
Mailing Address: 12901 Saw Mill Road, Louisville KY, 40272

ISBN 978-0-9826722-3-5
Linefork Publishing, 2011

Special thanks to Phillip Hartsock, whose formatting skills are almost as good as his singing.

to gardeners from here to there, especially:

Maureen, AJ, Meghan and Benjamin Conner, Whitney, Mom and Dad, Donald Conner, Sue Cox, Debby Matney, Chuck And Jackie Conner, Linda Smith, David Conner, Colleen and Phillip Hartsock, Felder Rushing, Betty Mackey, the Master Gardeners of Mercer County, PA, the Garden Writers Association, and my extended family on Facebook and Twitter, and all the others who've influenced how and why I plant and grow stuff.

Through The Seasons

FOREWORD.. 11

THE ILLUSTRATOR... 13

PREFACE... 15

INTRODUCING: THE WRITE GARDENER...................... 17

PART I - WINTER... 21

Snow-b-Gone..22

Heave Ho..25

Spring Song..29

Herbs of the Advent Wreath..33

Fruity Hillbilly Tomatoes...37

PART II - SPRING.. 41

Magicicada...43

Jolly Jonquils...47

Hands-on Gardening...52

Gardenologist...54

White House Garden..58

King Arthur's Scrubby Shrubbery..................................63

Out of the New, Into the Old..70

Through The Seasons

PART III - SUMMER 73

Lazy Gardening 74

Lawn Love 78

Herbs and Pawpaws 82

Bulbs, Tubers, Corms and Rhizomes 85

In the Zone 91

Dirt or Soil? 97

PART IV - FALL 101

Clean it Up 102

Politically Correct Gardening 106

Techno-gardening 110

Botanically Speaking 114

Falling for Mums 119

Individuality 124

Seasonal Gardening Tips 126

Why I Don't Cook 135

GLOSSARY 139

EPILOGUE 145

Bottle Tree
(Photo by Felder Rushing)

Foreword

You are holding in your hands something precious: Honest thoughts and humble admissions from a real gardener rambling around in a real garden.

Unlike big, beautiful "coffee table" garden books with their blow-dried photos, and presumptuous "how-to" advice manuals from preening horticulturists with all their rules, this is down-home observations and tips gleaned from years of sweat from gardening in summer heat and handling winter chores, and the hopes and pining and worries that come from doing real stuff in a real garden. And all which goes with it.

On the snowy day when I first met Terry Conner, casually known to his many friends as TC, he was sitting on the front row of an auditorium where I was about to give a lecture. As I checked the stage setup, TC's bright eyes and mischievous grin lured me down off the stage for a pre-lecture chat. Within minutes we were soul brothers, lifelong friends sharing anecdotes and kidding each other about gardening and life and kids. He changed my entire approach that day and for years to come, somehow making me more real than I had been on my own. A couple of years later he even helped me set up my very first digital presentation!

Though TC and I live and garden a thousand miles and several hardiness zones apart, we have visited one another numerous times (me in his snow, and he in my Deep South muggy humidity). I used his home and garden as "ground zero" for one of my own books, during which his practical gardening approach, Master Gardener training, and membership in the Garden Writers

Association helped make my book more readable and believable. I am still proud that he even wrote a rollicking but gracious foreword for the book.

I have watched TC and Maureen's two wonderful children grow up into refreshing young adults, helped wash up after TCs kitchen messes, divided hostas with him, painted flower pots we made out of inside-out tires, followed him through his years at Slippery Rock University, and shared rooms for economy at garden shows. We have also shared buckets of fried chicken in our trucks while driving back roads in search of interesting twists in "garden variety" gardens.

Through it all, his eager curiosity, humorous but sage insights, and natural abilities to share with others has culminated into this book of essays and observations from one of America's coolest, and most down-to-earth garden writers.

Ramble on!   – *Felder Rushing*

Felder and his traveling truck garden

Through The Seasons

The Illustrator

There's a photograph somewhere of my brother Don when he was around 12 or 13 years old. He's smiling proudly and holding a kite he made that won a contest. I don't remember the actual event as I was only six or seven at the time, but someone in the family told me it was held where my father worked, Belknap Hardware, in Louisville, Kentucky. I'll have to ask Don if he remembers any of the details. It's evident in the photo that Don has a very special talent, and it's never left him. Just flip through a few of these pages and the illustrations will attest to it.

There's something very special about Don's illustrations and oil paintings – Jesus is in each of them, if you look closely you'll see. It's Don's way of letting us know that as Christians we sometimes have to take a closer look. There's plenty of analogies and metaphors in Don's simple testimonial, but isn't it neat and so true that that's how it really is? Looking closer brings us closer and it reminds me of an old traditional gospel tune, here's a few lines: "Just a closer walk with Thee / Grant it, Jesus, is my plea / Daily walking close to Thee / Let it be, dear Lord, let it be."

Don and his wife Tonia experienced a tragedy recently when they lost their house and most all of their belongings in a fire. They're on the road to recovery now, the new house is up and they're settling in and beginning to make it feel like home again. When I first thought about asking him for illustrations for "Through the Seasons" I wasn't quite sure he'd do it, how could I expect him to after what happened? But Don said yes, and during the process had to take a little closer look within to get it done.

You might not be able to find Jesus in some of the illustrations here due to resizing, but He is in all of the originals. And guess what, He's there with you right now, if you don't know it, just look a little closer.

Through The Seasons

Preface

It's been a dream of mine to publish a book, specifically one about gardening. But with so much information available online, it almost seems pointless. The gardening books I've collected over the years are scattered around my workroom in shelves, on the floor under my desk – most of them unread. For some, collecting books on the subject may only be part of the gardening experience, and the actual reading of them is never accomplished. For garden writers, having them on hand for research purposes is very important. Even though I can easily Google, Bing, Ask.com, Facebook, Twitter, or Digg it, having a book in my hands with real pages is, at times, better than what technology offers.

Having said that, what follows is a compilation of what I consider to be my best articles. But of course using the personal pronoun "I" brings with it a large dose of subjective reasoning. It is hoped that this collection will provide you with pertinent information that can be taken outside and tossed onto the garden. It is best if the gardener then tills this under to a depth of eight or ten inches, after which soil amending might or might not be complete. It is not my intent to offer an absolute gardening information package within the covers of this book; that would be an encyclopedic undertaking. However, there are plenty of tips, tricks, and techniques that you can use to help you become a better gardener. And that's what this book is all about.

Through The Seasons

Editing was kept to a bare minimum throughout, and if you come across anything that just doesn't make sense I hope to be hearing from you. My contact information can be found on the last page and if you send me a question please include info on how I can get back in touch with you. If you spot a grammar or spelling error, an inaccuracy or oddity, an "i" without a dot or uncrossed "t," please let me know about them too.

Through The Seasons

Personal introductions that are included in most gardening books aren't about gardening, they're about the garden writer or in this case, me; TC, "The Write Gardener." I wrote my first article sometime in 2003, I was in my third semester of college, 46 years young, and had hopes to become a nationally recognized garden writer after I got my degree. The headline for my first article read: "Gardening column debuts" and I figured to be nationally recognized in no time. I'm 55 now, and still figuring.

Introducing: The Write Gardener

G A R D E N – what's the first thought that comes to your mind when you read that word? For most folks, I would say that it's probably images of vegetables, perhaps corn, tomatoes, or beans all set in straight and narrow rows, standing tall in the summer sun. But there's so much more to a garden besides vegetables. My mind's eye sees a beautiful red rose, in full bloom. If I think on it hard enough, I can almost smell the aroma. Others might picture a yard full of that little yellow and frilly bloomer some call a weed, the common dandelion. It appears en masse every year, whether we want it to or not. I have seen lawns that were completely covered with what looked like a giant yellow blanket; beautiful, I think. But before I get too carried away talking about gardening, I'd like to introduce myself; there will be more time for garden talk in future columns.

Through The Seasons

My name is Terry Conner; folks call me "TC" for short. I've been married to Maureen, the greatest woman on Earth, for 20 years. She and I have brought two children into the world, A.J., our 18-year old son, and Meghan, our daughter (my little sweetie-pie), is 16-years old. We live very modestly, in a big old house, on a big old lot, with plenty of room in the backyard for the gardens. There's even a little section of woods here that I like to think of as being mine (I don't think anyone really "owns" the land, we just borrow it a while).

I was born in a city much like Pittsburgh – Louisville, Kentucky, only it has one river running through it, not three. When I was fifteen my family moved to Greensburg, a small town located in the heart of the Bluegrass state. There you can find rolling hills, lonesome valleys, and a special place down a long gravel road that we called Tucker Holler.

It was there at Tucker Holler that not only my thumbs, but also my fingers and toes became green. Mom and Dad grew vegetables, lots of vegetables: potatoes, sweet corn, cucumbers, watermelons, green beans, and tomatoes, you name it and they probably grew it. It was the vegetable garden that sparked my interest in gardening. Although I now find it hard to understand how digging potatoes during the hot and humid Kentucky summers could create in me a love for gardening. I guess I could have rebelled against all that sweat and hard work, but it was the cold watermelon I ate on hot summer days, the bacon, lettuce, and tomato sandwiches, the fresh green beans and potatoes, and all the other fresh vegetables I helped to harvest that made it all worthwhile.

We grow mostly flowers here at our home in Pennsylvania, which can be more or less challenging than growing vegetables. Plenty of sweat and hard work is still required, and I've noticed that as I've aged, gardening is more challenging. But at least the humidity here isn't near as bad as it is in Kentucky and I try to grow flowers that don't require a lot of maintenance and attention. We still grow a few of our favorite vegetables, just enough for the family table. I love and need color in the garden and growing flowers meets and exceeds that need much more than growing vegetables.

Mother told me that her mom grew beautiful flowers, a special one that was always present in her summer garden – cosmos; it's now one of my favorite annuals. They're easy to grow from seed, don't require any special conditions, and when cut and used in a bouquet they're one of the best flowers for retaining freshness. I've had them in bouquets for over a week, looking almost as fresh as the day they were cut. My grandmother grew many other kinds of flowers and plants, and it was rumored that she could even grow a stick of firewood if she wanted to.

My hope is that you find my weekly articles informative and helpful. And together I think we can learn how to grow firewood, after all, firewood comes from trees and trees are plants.

Even after introductions, it can still seem awkward for some folks to talk to each other until they get better acquainted. First time gardeners and their gardens are like that too. You don't know what that seed will do, or how it will react to you once it sprouts (if it sprouts). And your garden might not like the way you tilled or turned it, and did you amend its soil correctly? It shouldn't take but a season or two for you and your garden to become best pals, and that's when the fun really starts. Beginnings are like introductions, and I think I'll begin my book with the winter season. That's the hardest season a gardener has to deal with, so let's get it out of the way first. It's also a good time for beginners to prepare themselves for what's to come.

Eastern Cardinal

Part I - Winter

Through The Seasons

After 22 years of living through winters in the northeast I've still not adjusted to the difference. Being a south-central Kentucky native, I wasn't used to weather forecasts that called for snow just about each and every day from December throughout March and on into April and sometimes May. But for northerners, dealing with snow every winter is as normal as southerners dealing with heat and humidity (humidity "so thick you can lick it," southern garden writer Felder Rushing says) each and every summer. It's that time of year dear gardening friends, when snow is falling, ice is forming, and we're worried if the kids will play with their Christmas toys for more than a week. You should also be concerned with using safe amounts of ice-melt salt on the front walkway. Runoff from chemically treated snowy sidewalks can be dangerous to our landscape plants. Before you begin tossing handfuls of salty chemicals on sidewalks and patios, make sure you know which types are harmful and which aren't.

Snow-b-Gone

The majority of de-icing salts contain calcium chloride. Calcium chloride produces heat when introduced to water thereby lowering the melting or freezing point. This is termed "freezing point depression" by chemists and has something to do with the "colligative property" of water (i.e., the number of particles in a liquid or solvent). Before this turns into a chemistry class, let's just say that more particles mean more melting power.

More particles and more melting power in salts for snow and ice removal might be fine for large applications such as parking lots and interstate highways. But homeowners should never use industrial strength ice melts around their landscape plants. Ice melt products for home use are distilled into a mix of four compounds of chloride: sodium, calcium, magnesium and potassium chlorides, amounts of each are strictly controlled.

As with all chemical applications, knowing how much to use is a must. Labeling will provide you with application rates, and should also state precautions, storage instructions, and manufacturer contact information. Keep in mind that the effectiveness of ice and snow melting products is based on several factors, including but not limited to: amount of snow or ice, amount of sun or shade, surface temperature, and effectiveness for a given temperature range. The use of different products may be preferable depending on the temperature. Check labels for products that are most effective for zone 5 average winter temperatures (about 30 degrees, give or take a few).

You'll also find liquid de-icers effective against ice and snow. If the air temperature or the temperature of the surface you want to de-ice is below freezing water may be unavailable to dissolve granular ice melting products, this reduces its effectiveness. Liquid de-icers aren't widely available to homeowners yet so you might have to do some legwork.

Regardless of solid or liquid form, neither will be effective if it's too cold. When temperatures fall below five degrees, you might be tempted to use extreme amounts, don't; it's wasteful and might harm or even kill plants. If it's bitterly cold, the best thing to do is nothing. Whatever you use and whenever you use it use less. You just need to get the melting process started, do this by adding small amounts and then wait till it's all dissolved to add any more. You can even pre-apply before snow arrives to stay on top of things.

So, what's the safest thing you can use to melt ice and snow on walkways near the garden, lawns, and other plantings? There is no guarantee, but following label directions to the letter and using less product will help prevent most chemicals from harming your ornamental plants and shrubs. And of course there's always the completely chemical-free thing called a shovel.

It's good to keep a collection of gardening tips out by the potting shed. If I had saved all the tips from day one, there would probably be enough to fill a book. I didn't though, but it's never too late to start. I might even come up with enough to fill a book. (Or at least a section at the back of this one.)

Heaving is a term most southerners probably never heard of. But northerners are most familiar with the occurrence. It doesn't happen all the time, but if you garden where winters are cold and long it's something you should be aware of.

Heave Ho

I guess I should've put the snowplow blade on a couple of weeks ago during that short warm spell we had. I figured I would get around to it before any significant snowfall, but I was wrong. Maureen says she feels like she's in a slushy figure-8 race trying to drive the car the short distance to the garage once she turns in the driveway. So now I find myself looking forward to spending half a day out in the cold garage wrestling with that contraption. Mississippi garden writer Felder Rushing says, "You know you're a northern gardener if your riding mower has a snow plow attachment," well, I reckon Felder knew what he was talking about. So I guess I should get on out there and attach mine. Maureen will be thankful.

We all know that sometimes winter weather patterns can have us longing for an early spring, especially after witnessing one or two days when temperatures are well into the 60s. In reality, Nature

Through The Seasons

has to keep us snow-covered for a while longer so that northern gardeners can stay in tune with the seasons. There are things we need to be aware of when short warm blasts move into the area after the ground has frozen. Heaving is one of those things.

Folks that garden in warmer climes don't have to worry about heaving. But it's a known phenomenon that sometimes occurs here in the northeast. What actually happens is a lifting of frozen ground caused by thawing. Roots may be exposed on some plants and this can lead to damage.

It's a good idea to take a tour of your garden after a January thaw and look for heaving. If you notice this condition, gently push the soil back down and around the roots of your plant. If heaving has caused complete root exposure, carefully push the roots down into the soil and add at least a three or four inch layer of mulch. If your plants' roots haven't been exposed to the elements very long, they should survive.

Besides heaving of soil around your plants and shrubs, also be aware of upheavals around concrete and stonework in paths. If you use ice melt, use it sparingly around flowerbeds. Sodium chloride is the chemical used in ice melting materials and if too much "Ice-B-Gone" is used, your plants may be gone too come spring.

Sodium causes soil compaction and inhibits root growth and excessive amounts can prevent plants from absorbing nutrients from the soil. Penn State Cooperative Extension agent Melanie

Through The Seasons

Barkley says using small amounts of garden fertilizer will melt ice. "The potash portion, the third number on the fertilizer label (K – potassium), is the ice melter. It is not as effective as salt, but in small quantities it can be used by the plants next spring," she said.

Snow is a great insulator and is effective in helping keep your plants safe from winter heaving. It can also weigh heavily on the boughs and branches of shrubs and ornamental trees. To help prevent breakage, it's a good idea to remove excess snow. (Try to do this while one of your kids happens to be standing under the snow-covered branch. Tell them you didn't know they were there.)

In keeping with the tradition of Groundhog Day, I offer up this little poem.

Punxsutawney Phil please pay attention.
You're out of your hole, you've made your prediction.
Whether it's sunny or whether it's gray,
when speaking your groundhogese I hoped you'd say:
"An earlier spring is what I now see.
All northern gardeners can order more seeds.
Remove those snowplows attached to your mowers,
I say winter snows will be melting, they're over!"
But I find myself doubting your forecasting powers.
And if your divination turns out to be weeds in my flowers,
I'll not say a word, nor hold it against you.
Because you're only a groundhog and it's the best you could do.

Winters in the northeast are a time for hibernating, and not only for critters like groundhogs. But my hibernating mode is quite different from a groundhog's; instead of sleeping away the winter, I suffer from gardening withdrawal through most of my waking hours. On a more serious note, winters can cause a condition known as Seasonal Affective Disorder that can be quite a problem for some folks. I deal with it the best I can, and so far I've succeeded in making it through 21 northeastern winters.

Through the Seasons

I can't find my copy of Monty Don's book <u>Gardening Mad</u>, and I'm mad! I used it when I wrote the following article but now it's disappeared. Catholics know of Saint Anthony, the Patron Saint of Lost Things, and often pray "Saint Anthony, Saint Anthony please come around, something's lost and must be found." Gardening columnist for the London newspaper "The Observer," Monty Don's book inspired me to write mine. His collection of articles was about gardening in England, I've never been, but hear it's rainy, damp, and chilly most of the time. I suppose gardeners there are used to it.

Spring Song

The opening day of hunting season brought temperatures in the high fifties, much to the dismay of Pennsylvania deer hunters. And I have a strong urge to till the garden and plant it again. Ahhh, November in western Pennsylvania, as a friend of mine used to say, "It don't get any better!" And as Mother still says, "It could be worse."

For the past several days, daytime temperatures have topped fifty degrees, giving gardeners reason to be hoping for an early spring. But I'd be willing to bet a Yankee dime that November will end on a snowy note, giving the cold shoulder to our hopes for an early spring, for now anyway.

But that is as it should be and the passing of the season allows the garden a period of rest and rejuvenation. That seems pleasureless to us for our pleasure comes from what's visible during the growing season and from what we do to achieve success as gardeners. It's the lush greens, yellows, and burgundys of the vegetables and flowers we grow, it's the taste of homegrown tomatoes, beans, and corn that provide rewards equal to any pirate's chest full of crown jewels.

The winter solstice occurs precisely at 7:22 pm EST on December 21, marking the shortest day and the longest night of the year. Following the winter solstice, the days begin to lengthen and the nights get shorter. It's the lengthening days that is most anticipated by gardeners. We take pleasure in knowing the days are growing longer because we see it as a sign of Nature progressing as she should, bringing the spring thaw in on schedule.

While I wait for spring's song to return, I often wonder what happens beneath the garden during winter. Are worms digging their way deeper, finding warmer areas to settle into? What else takes place under the frozen layer of soil while we wait for an above ground thaw? Are voles and moles hibernating or feasting on your crocus and tulip bulbs? Probably feasting, both are active

Through the Seasons

throughout the winter months. (Voles eat plants, moles eat insects.)

Isn't it quite amazing how perennials return to their glorious state of bloom after lying dormant and, to put it bluntly, ugly for so long? This is not something new, it's been happening just this way since God made dirt. But how often do you stop and think about it during the growing season, once or twice, maybe? Monty Don writes elegantly in "Gardening Mad" about the winter garden:

"You could be forgiven for not noticing any spanking changes appearing outside and the garden can still seem Pompeian, locked inside a volcanic casing of cold and grey light, but things are getting better. The days are getting longer for a start and it is surprising how quickly that shows. And quietly, quietly, there are happenings. The garden might be in a coma but beneath the sullen skin the heart is beating strongly. I love to think of plants growing underground, showing nothing above the abrasive knobbliness of frozen earth, but secretly pushing out tentative roots and new roots, blind and mole-like but unstoppable."

Yes Mr. Don, the garden will erupt, as Mount Vesuvius did so long ago when it destroyed the city of Pompeii. But when it does the only thing it might destroy will be my hopes of a weedless garden. And I won't mind that, because weeds in my garden are as much a part of it as the root system of my finest rose.

So I wait for the real urge to arrive, the one that tells me it's time to plant, the one that's triggered by an early spring thaw.

Through the Seasons

Many thanks to the county's road crews for keeping the snow cleared from major roadways. The only complaint I have is the massive pile up of snow at the end of my driveway. It makes for a tough exit and entry, unless I keep it cleared using my mower as a snow plow. Some winters bring more snow than others, and I always hope for less but usually get more.

Christmas is a special time, and even though it's often commercialized to the point of silliness, Christmas will often bring out the best in everyone. And I think God grows mostly herbs in His garden.

Herbs of the Advent Wreath

Sometime around the 6th Century BCE, Church fathers recognized the liturgical year, which determined when feasts, memorials and commemorations are to be observed and which portions of Scripture are to be read. This started the Christian tradition of Advent. The season of Advent is a holy season of the Christian church, the period of preparation for the celebration of the birth of Christ. It is the beginning of the Christian year.

There are four Sundays in Advent traditionally celebrated with four candles, often on an Advent wreath, with one to be lit each Sunday. Three of the candles are violet, or purple, and one is rose-colored or pink. Purple symbolizes faithful expectation, and pink symbolizes joy and hope. A taller fifth candle, usually white, is sometimes placed in the center of the Advent wreath to be lit on Christmas Day signifying Christ's birth.

My wife, Maureen, has been making beautiful wreaths ever since I've known her. For those of you wondering when we first met, I believe the year was 1988, or was it 1989? Anyway, she uses evergreen clippings from arborvitae, boxwood, holly, juniper

Through the Seasons

and pine or spruce trees growing here in our backyard. She says most anything showing green growth is perfectly fine to use in a wreath. That is if you know how to make them. I'm not too adept at it myself, there are some things she's much better at than I am, wreath making and memorizing important dates, such as our anniversary, are two perfect examples.

Our Advent wreath is displayed on the living room table and during our Small Faith Group meeting the other evening I noticed the distinct odor of sage emanating from somewhere near the table. I looked at the wreath and saw the addition of several herbs in with the other evergreens, sage being one of them. I'm always interested in discovering new uses for plants and this time my nose told me of another use.

Medieval times saw the use of herbs for many things, so it shouldn't be surprising for them to be used in Advent wreaths today. Maureen attended an herbal wreath-making workshop at *Crystalaire Herbscapes* in Harrisville and decided it was time she started using the aromatic plants in her Advent wreaths. I'm glad she chose to incorporate herbs into our displays of greenery around the house.

If you decide it's time for the herbal Advent wreath in your home, the following herbs should be considered for their aroma and their special symbolic meaning during the upcoming Christmas season.

✓ Bedstraw (*Galium verum*) – Often called "Our Lady's

Bedstraw" because legend says it was the manger hay for the Christ Child, bedstraw blooms in late June and into July. Harvest this herb just as its golden clusters of miniature flowers open. Hang them to dry in a dark room for later use in your Advent wreath.

Boxwood (*Buxus longifolia*) – Boxwood symbolizes long life and immortality and has been used for decorating churches and other places of worship for many years. Found growing in mountainous regions of Palestine, and the Galilean hills, boxwoods are hardy to zone five and can grow to 25 feet. Most gardeners keep this evergreen trimmed well below that height and its use as miniature hedges in borders is popular.

✓ Juniper (*Juniperus communis*) – Traditionally used in the sanctuary, juniper signifies life and hope. Its use in wreaths and garlands dates back centuries, when it was also placed on windows and doorsills to protect occupants from evil. Its sweet fragrance is indicative of Christmas.

✓ Lavender (*Lavandula*) – Symbolizing purity and virtue, lavender is perhaps this writer's favorite among the aromatic plants in the herbal family. Some claim that lavender is the spikenard mentioned in St. Mark's Gospel when Jesus visits the leper, "And being in Bethany in the house of Simon the leper, as he sat at meat, there came a woman having an alabaster box of ointment of spikenard very precious; and she brake the box, and poured it on his head." (Mark 14:3) The clean and fresh aroma of lavender is certainly welcome indoors through the winter months, and having a bundle dried for wreath making and adding to potpourri is an essential part of Maureen's herbal crafting.

✓ Sage (*Salvia officinalis*) – Symbolizing immortality, sage grows well in zones 4-9 and likes full sun. Dry sage as you would other herbs. I strung a very simple "clothesline" in our meager kitchen from which now hangs bunches of sage, and other herbs and flowers. Common sage has blue flowers that grow on short, straight spires. Leaves are soft and silvery green with a finely pebbled texture.

Sometimes our sense of smell is a big memory booster. Sage and other aromatic herbs bring back childhood memories of warm kitchens and a turkey roasting in the oven. Maureen says rosemary has special medicinal qualities that enhance memorization. Perhaps I should ask my doctor if there's a prescription strength variety.

Through the Seasons

If it were decreed that gardeners could grow only one vegetable, I would pick the tomato. Funny thing though, tomatoes are not vegetables.

Fruity Hillbilly Tomatoes

Maureen and I were mulling over the seeds we'll be starting next month and the subject of vegetables came up. Maureen posited that if you ask someone if they garden, many would probably say, "Oh, we just grow a few tomatoes." This just goes to show how popular the tomato (Solanum *lycopersicum*) really is. Folks I know who don't have a backyard garden plot will more often than not grow a tomato plant or three strategically placed in a section of dirt close to the back door. "If people were to grow only one thing, it's going to be tomatoes," Maureen said.

You might say tuh-MAH-toe, and I might say tuh-MAY-toe, but how did this vegetable that isn't really a vegetable (more on that later) get to be so popular? Besides sunflowers, the most prominent plant that pops into my mind when I think of summer is a tomato plant; one laden with big, fat, juicy, heirloom ugly tomatoes! President Jefferson helped popularize tomatoes in the

U.S. after biting into one in Paris in the late 1700s, shortly afterwards he began growing his own at Monticello.

It's hard to pinpoint exactly where the tomato came from. However,

major work conducted by Russian botanist Nikolai Vavilov (1887-1943) identified a "centres of origin" of cultivated plants which led to the idea that if one wants to locate the very center of origin for any crop species, look for the area which still has the highest diversity of that crop. For the tomato, Vavilov found that area to be off the western coast of South America in present day Peru where eight species in the tomato genus still grow wild in the Andes Mountains.

During the 18th and 19th centuries, the tomato experienced intense domestication throughout much of the civilized world. It was discovered that most cultivars self-pollinated which meant that cross-cultivation rarely occurred. Tomatoes grown from seed of such plants resembled the parent plant and at the time, a lot of high quality tomatoes were being produced in Europe. With this realization came even more domestication as farmers and gardeners began saving seed from their "heirloom" tomato plants. Heirlooms dating back over a hundred years are still grown today.

I owe a lot of thanks to Gary Millwood, an heirloom tomato gardener in Louisville, Kentucky, for introducing me to several new varieties of heirloom tomatoes. Our friendship began several years ago via a Dave's Garden web post about tomatoes. I was seeking information about heirlooms because I'd heard about their superior taste. Gary replied with lots of info and I knew immediately that he was a tomato expert. It was shortly after this that I discovered Pittsburgh's own heirloom tomato 'Potato Top.' Three years later, and now I only grow heirloom tomatoes. They may not be as photogenic as hybrids, but what they lack in appearance, they more than make up for in taste.

I mentioned earlier that tomatoes aren't vegetables; scientifically they're considered fruits and here's the simple reason why: seeds. So, this means that since most other vegetables we grow in the garden have seeds, for example cucumbers and squash, they must be fruit too. Yes, they are. If you can answer the question "Does it have seeds?" with yes, then you have a fruit. Most everything else can be grouped into the vegetable category – radishes, celery, carrots, etc. You might wonder about potatoes since they're in the same family (Solanum) as tomatoes. Do they have seeds? No. Potatoes are considered to be root crops, or tuberous vegetables.

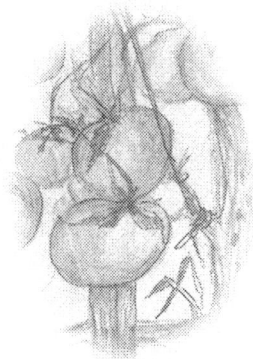

Heirloom or hybrid, we are a particular bunch when it comes to which variety of tomato we like to grow. Some say the earlier ripening varieties such as Beefsteak and Early Girl are their top choice and others patiently wait for late season heirloom favorites like 'Abe Lincoln' or Brandywine. Perhaps my friend Gary sums it up best when he talks about why he loves growing heirloom tomatoes:

Through the Seasons

"What I think is important as I consider each individual story of these tomato varieties is that someone thought they had some good qualities and made attempts to save seed. Many were shared with family, friends and others. Each time I discover a variety like one of these, it is like discovering a 'lost' treasure. The growing and the tasting provide experiences others have encountered over the years. For me it reminds me of blissful summers and cold winters when soups and sauces warmed the heart bringing back memories of boyhood days long ago."

It may not seem like a reason for growing heirloom tomatoes, but a lot of us choose varieties based on names like 'Hillbilly,' 'Black Mountain Pink,' 'Purple Dog Creek,' 'Cherokee Purple,' or 'Grandma Oliver's Green.' It's easy to see the popularity of these deliciously named heirloom tomatoes.

We've been growing mostly heirloom tomatoes for several years. They're susceptible to most every disease you can name, take longer to mature, require more staking, and are just plain ugly to look at when ripe. And yet we absolutely couldn't do without them. Just thinking about and choosing the varieties we'll grow helps me make it through the long northeast winters.

Part II - Spring

Bugs are a necessary part of life and we shouldn't try to eliminate every single one we see crawling around in the garden. If there were no bugs, there'd be no humans either. Some bugs only appear once in a blue moon, or even wait longer than that. There's a very strange story in the Old Testament about a plague of locusts that a certain pharaoh had to endure, I wonder if they were cicadas?

Magicicada

It's time for the periodic cicada to awaken from its long nap. The last time these ominous looking insects appeared was 1987. I was in Cincinnati, Ohio visiting my cousin Larry on Memorial Day, and I remember Larry's wife, Donna, going outside to check the burgers on the grill and getting dive-bombed by cicadas. At least that's what she thought was happening. When they emerge there are so many of them that they often fly into each other causing mid-air crashes.

What's so fascinating about the periodic cicadas, commonly but mistakenly referred to as locusts, is the fact that their 17-year cycle appearance occurs nowhere else in the world besides North America, particularly, the eastern half of the United States, where they are a native species. Pennsylvania is one of 14 states expected to be inundated with cicadas sometime around the middle of this month when mature nymphs start tunneling their way to the surface of the soil. They then wait for some predetermined signal from Mother Nature before venturing out and climbing up the nearest tree trunk, wee, or other vertical object. My legs are vertical when I'm standing, and they're objects. Do you think...? No, surely they wouldn't mistake a human leg for a tree trunk, would they?

I wouldn't worry too much if you do happen to have a close encounter of the cicada kind when they show up. Cicadas are completely harmless to humans. They may cause some damage to young trees with small branches as the females lay their eggs but you can minimize damage by wrapping the tree trunk with row cover or cheese cloth. If you have fruit tree orchards other precautions such as chemical control methods may be considered. Read and follow safety directions on labels and call a professional or contact your local county extension office if you have any questions about using pesticides. (Mercer County Extension Office: 724-662-3141.)

Gregory Hoover, Senior Extension Associate with Penn State's Department of Entomology states that "soon after emerging, males begin their constant 'singing' while females remain silent. The sound made by an adult male is sometimes haunting and eerie," and also very, very loud!

Through the Seasons

Penn State offers detailed information about the periodic cicada in their *Entomological Notes* publication. Hoover offers the following additional information regarding the periodic cicada:

About 10 days after emergence, females will mate and begin depositing eggs in twigs and branches of nearly 80 different preferred species of trees and woody shrubs. They usually do not deposit eggs in coniferous trees. Generally, the female will deposit 400-600 eggs in the twigs of the preferred species. Using the blades of a saw-like, egg-laying device at the end of the abdomen, females puncture the bark of a twig and make a pocket in the wood. Females may deposit 24-28 eggs in two rows in one of these pockets. They then move forward, cut another pocket and lay more eggs. The pockets are placed close together in a straight row sometimes forming a continuous slit for two to three inches.

Adults live for approximately three to four weeks above ground. Most are usually gone by the beginning of July. Hatching occurs six to seven weeks after egg laying, and the white, antlike nymphs work their way out of the slits and drop to the ground where they enter the soil. Here they insert their piercing-sucking mouthparts and draw plant fluid from roots of plants for the next 17 years. (Hoover's detailed report can be found on the web at: http://ento.psu.edu/extension/factsheets/periodical-cicada?searchterm=periodic%2520cicada)

Through the Seasons

By the way, today is my birthday and I may have a few thousand cicadas here to help me celebrate. It's been 17 years since I saw these intriguing insects and their arrival coinciding with my birthday should make for an interesting party.

The periodic cicada invasion for the year mentioned (2004) was a bust. I think I might have seen six or eight of them. But other regions not far from here had them crawling everywhere. 1987 at my cousin's house in Cincinnati was something to behold. It was much like the tale of the plague of locusts mentioned in the Bible, which seems to reinforce the Truth of the Good Book, at least in my mind.

Through the Seasons

Nothing shouts "spring!" louder than a hillside or yard full of daffodils. I should have a yard full but don't. I keep saying I'll add more one of these days, but I never do. What is it that prevents us from doing the things that we say we're going to do? If I knew the answer I'd have a yard full of daffs!

Jolly Jonquils

In Greek mythology, Narcissus was a hero acclaimed for his beauty. There are several versions of the myth, all of which relate a tale about how Narcissus was so enamored with his own beauty that he couldn't tell his reflection apart from his real self. Narcissism, named after Narcissus, is a form of vanity and today it's mostly used to describe arrogance, smugness, self-love or some other not-so-attractive trait in humans.

The lovely yellow spring flowering daffodil is also named after Narcissus. Perhaps due to another Greek tale that says the narcissus flower was created to lure Demeter's daughter Persephone away from her friends so that Hades could kidnap her. Demeter was the Greek goddess of agriculture, Persephone was the Queen of the Underworld of epic literature, and Hades was the god of the underworld.

This is supposed to be a gardening column, not a lesson in

Greek mythology, but I couldn't think of a better segue to use in order to introduce what is arguably the most recognizable of all spring flowers; recognizable only in bloom, unless you're a bulb expert. Daffodils are a bulbous plant and a bulb is "a food storage organ consisting of fleshy scales attached to a basal plate, often within a papery tunic," (so says The American Horticultural Society A-Z Encyclopedia of Garden Plants).

Gardeners plant all kinds of spring flowering bulbs. Besides daffodils, other common bulbous plants you might catch a glimpse of now are crocus and tulips. Daffodils are categorized into 13 descriptive divisions with Trumpet cultivars in division 1 being very prominent here in our neck of the woods. The American Daffodil Society's Web site provides photographs of daffs from each division (daffodilusa.org).

Depending on the time of season (early, mid, and late), daffs bloom on leafless stems bearing anywhere from 1 to 20 flowers. Flowers have 6 petals surrounding a long narrow cup. Botanically speaking, perianth is petals and the cup is the corona. Division identification is based on coloring, size, and texture of perianth and corona.

I'd leave it up to the pros if you're trying to identify a daff that's been flowering in the backyard every spring for the past 20 years. With hundreds of differing color hues of yellow and white, identifying a specific plant is guesswork for those of us who don't know any better. (Unless you saved the label from the mesh bag,

Through the Seasons

and even then it's iffy, sometimes the label doesn't state the variety name.)

"Arrayed in waves across the garden or setting a hillside on yellow fire, daffodils seem to generate their own light," writes Dora Galitzki in Martha Stewart Living (April, 2005). Indeed, a drive into Mercer from Grove City on Rt. 58 will take you by Vicki and Andy Narlee's place where a hillside on fire has been re-igniting with daffs every spring since forever according to Andy. This is probably due to naturalizing. At some point, previous owners planted a handful or two along the bank and over the years the bulbs multiplied, giving present owners Andy and his wife Vicki a bank worthy of robbing. Which Andy says has happened on occasion: "I've noticed clumps missing from time to time. People will stop and dig up a bunch and drive off." Andy says that he has nothing against folks stopping to take pictures, or pick a handful for the vase. But please, do not dig up someone else's flowers unless they tell you it's okay (I have mint for immediate removal, come dig all you want).

Most daffodils are hardy to zone 3 and there are many varieties to choose from. Specialty bulb catalogs such as Brent and Becky's Bulbs carry just about every size, shape, and hue of yellow you could want, plus their Web site lists growing specifications by division (www.brentandbeckysbulbs.com). When choosing your daffs, think about spacing out bloom time by planting a few of each type: early, mid, and late season varieties.

Through the Seasons

'Rijnveld's Early Sensation' for the early show and 'Chromacolor' for the late show are two picks to pique your interest.

Plant narcissus in fall at a depth three to four times the height of the bulb. Daffodils grow their roots in autumn when soil temperature at planting depth falls below 60 degrees. This is why most planting is done after the first hard frost (don't be late and let the ground freeze before you get the bulbs in). Roots stop growing once the ground freezes but then restart in spring when the soil thaws. Daffs like good drainage so amend the soil accordingly before planting. They also need at least half a day's sunshine with waterings in fall and again in spring (if needed); dry summer weather does not affect daffodils.

Try a handful of your favorites along hillsides, planting them in groups of a dozen or so. A scattered effect in open spaces will turn more heads than daffs lined up like soldiers along a walkway. Daffs mix well with evergreen shrubs; use taller varieties in back and shorter ones in front. Plant groups of random shades for added color interest. Get daffy with your daffs and you'll feel springier in spring!

One more thing, in places south of the Mason-Dixon daffodils are commonly called jonquils. This is because of an early import of Narcissus jonquilla that was naturalized across a large area.

Through the Seasons

Atop Buckner Hill in the small town of Greensburg, Kentucky, there's a field of jonquil. It's been a favorite picture taking spot for many years. I used to live close to that flowery field, in a 12x60 foot trailer on a lot that had hillsides I had to mow. Those hillsides were so steep that I had to use a rope tied to the mower handle in order to mow them. I swore I'd never live on a lot like that ever again, and I haven't. I also haven't ever seen a field full of jonquil quite like the one on top of Buckner Hill.

Hands-on Gardening

Mrs. Barbara Bookwalter lives in western Pennsylvania and says she's "been gardening since, well, forever." Growing things in Pennsylvania's mostly clay soils can be a challenge for gardeners. Clay soils retain moisture and if you're not sure about a plant's ability to live in soggy soils, planting in clay could bring disappointment. Barb has held onto the knowledge and experience she learned as a child from a mother who taught her how to use her hands in the garden. "When I was little, we had a very large vegetable garden. Being the youngest of 8 children, we all shared the work," Barb recalls. Sharing the work, that's always good when you have plenty of hands to go around.

Barb remembers growing lots of vegetables and after her family harvested all they could use, any additional produce would be sold at a roadside stand. During harvest season in most rural areas of the country, you'll see quaint little wooden framed shacks with handmade signs, brightly painted: FRESH SWEET CORN - $4 A BAKER'S DOZEN. "Back then I considered gardening a chore. I grew up, got married and have three children of my own. Now I find gardening relaxing, a time to enjoy

nature and just think." Barb's take on garden work being relaxing is somewhat paradoxical. You might wonder how digging, pulling, hoeing, and raking can be relaxing; it's not, in the physical sense. But those with several years of gardening experience know the benefits that working hands can bring to an overworked mind – relaxation is a mighty fine benefit and that gray matter in our heads need it!

Through the Seasons

Spring continues to strengthen during the month of April. Its equinox in March doesn't really engage the gardening mind, not mine anyway. Many good things happen in April: my wedding anniversary, family birthdays, National Poetry Month, and as mentioned in the following article, National Gardening Month. Sometimes April fools us with weather warm enough to maybe do a little gardening, but I've come to rely more on June's weather to get me in the mood. June should be NGM.

Gardenologist

In honor of April being National Gardening Month, I declare all readers of this column gardenologists. You may officially christen yourself as such in two days. The first thing you must do as gardenologists is cease and desist from all cold thoughts, right now! And repeat the following five words (grammatically speaking, six words) out loud (it's okay to do this while you're at work, if someone is staring at you, ask them to join in): There's no place like home, there's no place... wait a minute, that's not it. There's no more cold weather, there's no more cold weather, there's no more cold weather.

Now, I bet you feel warmer already. I did after I repeated it, thanks in part to my good friend Felder Rushing who called while I was writing this and said the predicted high temperature was supposed to reach 81 degrees in his hometown of Jackson,

Through the Seasons

Mississippi. He does this just to tease me about his zone 8 garden. He warmed my blood even more when he said their shrub roses are budding out and the red bud trees are in full bloom. Later on that same evening I was instant messaging with my brother Chuck in Kentucky and he told me March lilies (daffodils) were blooming everywhere. By this time, my blood was boiling as I thought about what we have in bloom here: Nothing.

But as all good northeast gardenologists know, our planting and growing season is about a month behind Kentucky's and about two months behind Mississippi's. And we live in a part of the country that just doesn't have a lengthy growing season. So, we make do with what we have and enjoy our early spring blooming perennials such as crocus and daffodils all the more when they're finally showing off. Other early season spring blooming perennials that compliment the bulbs and help wake up the perennial garden include Lenten rose (Hellebores), crested iris (Iris cristata), lungwort (Pulmonaria saccharata), and a favorite of my sweetie pie's when she was toddling around the spring garden, violets (Viola spp.)

For instant color and to enhance the perennial beds, gardenologist Maureen pots up plenty of annuals. While visiting Buffalo Springs Herb Farm last summer, we spotted the gorgeously grape-colored Persian shield (*Strobilanthes dyerianus*).

Through the Seasons

Persian shield has very metallic foliage reflecting hues of copper and blue and makes a great container plant. I'm not sure if local nurseries will carry this plant but gardenologists can order it online at www.selectseeds.com. Along with Persian shield, consider the following annuals for your pots this summer:

- ✓ Ageratum (*Ageratum houstonianum*) 'Hawaii Sky Blue' is a Fleuroselect quality award winner and a top performer in containers. It has sky-blue flowers and grows to four inches.

- ✓ Begonia (*Begonia semperflorens*) 'Doublonia Red' has double red flowers and grows to eight inches. Begonia 'Queen White' would be the perfect companion for a fourth of July pairing of pots on the patio, along with Ageratum 'Hawaii Sky Blue.'

- ✓ Celosia (*Celosia argentea plumosa*) 'Fresh Look Red' was a gold medal winner for Fleuroselect in 2003. With its bold and spiky deep red flowers, containers of 'Fresh Look Red' will freshen up any walkway or garden path.

Besides container plantings, gardenologists love adding new plants to existing flowerbeds and old-fashioned hollyhocks (Alcea rosea) have been a favorite here for a long time. Hollyhocks are bi-annuals (a bi-annual is a plant that does not usually bloom its

first year after planting and will re-seed from spent flower heads, blooming in its second year of growth), and the recent (2003) addition of a dwarf variety is a welcome one. 'Queenie Purple' has frilly, light-purple double flowers, reaches 14 to 16 inches and grows best in full sun and moderately fertile, well-drained soil.

Gaillardia (*Gaillardia aristata*, common name, blanket flower) 'Arizona Sun' is a Fleuroselect gold medal winner with red and yellow daisy-like blooms. Its compact round form averages a height of eight inches, and can spread to 10. 'Arizona Sun' flowers from June to September and likes living in fertile, well-drained soil. I have a clump of blanket flower at the end of my driveway that stays covered in roadside slushy, highway-salt contaminated snow. It recovers yearly proving its durability as a tough-as-nails plant.

The term "gardenologist" does not exist. I made it up because it sounds important, like one of those words a horthead, biology or physiology professor would use. The suffix "ology" simply means "learned and knowledgeable in a certain field of study." So, if you want, go ahead and call yourself a gardenologist. I know y'all are learned and knowledgeable gardeners because you're reading my book!

Through the Seasons

I don't remember whose idea it was to put in a garden at The White House but it sure garnered a heck of a lot of attention, at first. The season progressed, the whoopla wore off, and you didn't hear anything more about it. I wonder if the President hoed, or if the First Lady watered? I understand that there's a large groundskeeping crew that does most of the gardening and landscaping around The White House, but I'm pretty sure that the President and First Lady do a little gardening too.

White House Garden

Garden writers everywhere have probably been pecking at their keyboards like hens at feeding time – The White House is putting in a new garden! It became official last Friday on a spot of lawn on the south side of the White House. Michele Obama and a group of fifth graders from a local elementary school in Washington gathered on the spot to do some general preparation work for the new garden.

There's been other White House gardens dating back to World War II when Eleanor Roosevelt prompted the nation to plant gardens to help the war effort, setting the perfect example, her's was the first "victory garden" planted in 1943. John Adams, our second President, had a garden,

Through the Seasons

Hilary Clinton had a rooftop container garden and Woodrow Wilson kept a flock of sheep grazing on the White House lawn.

Michele Obama's new White House garden comes at a time when we're seeing a 32% increase in the sale of fruit and vegetable plants, giving much credence to the claim that folks are starting to see the importance of growing their own produce in their own backyard gardens. For those of us who've been avid gardeners for years, hearing of a first family garden being started on the lawn of the White House is exciting news, but it's really old news being presented in a new era.

The United States Department of Agriculture (USDA) may have inspired the First Lady to start her new garden after Agriculture Secretary Tom Vilsack decided to "break pavement for the People's Garden." That announcement was made last month when the USDA decided it had 1,250 square feet of "unnecessary paved surface" at its headquarters in Washington. A USDA news release explains that the new People's Garden "will add 612 square feet of planted space to an existing garden traditionally planted with ornamentals." Secretary Vilsack envisions a "community garden at each USDA facility worldwide."

Getting back to Mrs. Obama's garden, it's been interesting to see the blogosphere's reaction to this new victory garden. Some bloggers seem to think Mrs. Obama might be too busy with her duties as First Lady to be bothered with mundane gardening chores such as weeding or hoeing. Others say it's not too farfetched to believe that we'll see her working in the garden along with her two daughters, Malia and Sasha. I'm inclined to believe that if Mrs. Obama decides to be active in the garden, she'll realize its calming effect and spend any extra time she might have working and relaxing in her new garden.

News reports say the First Lady has never had a vegetable garden before, if I could I'd love to verify that and then ask Mrs. Obama a few questions myself. I'm sure we'd all like to know if the President plans on getting his hands dirty. I'd also like to know if the Obamas realize the importance of us seeing them as having common interests like the rest of us. Sometimes I think we have a tendency to believe they don't.

So, what's being planted in the new White House veggie garden? Before answering that, I think I should point out that we're still waiting on seeds here so we can start what we'll be planting. I mentioned the increase in vegetable plant sales, and it must be true for seeds as well. I'm sure it's much easier for White House gardener Dale Haney to purchase seeds and plants. Oh well, the privilege of being the White House horticulturalist has its benefits I suppose.

As far as vegetables in the new White House garden, I noticed many of the same ones we all grow – lettuce, sugar snap peas, radishes, perennial and annual herbs like rosemary and cilantro, there's even a planting of rhubarb listed. It's a bit worrisome to me that there's no green bean variety shown, perhaps I should call White House Assistant Chef Sam Kass and extol the wonderful taste of 'Kentucky Wonder' pole beans.

White House gardener Dale Haney will implement organic gardening in the new garden and vegetables will be harvested for use in White House meals. Any extra produce will go to local area food banks. Raised beds in the new garden will be fertilized with crab meal from the Chesapeake Bay, lime and green sand. Predatory insects such as praying mantises will help keep unwanted bugs out of the new garden, and ladybugs will also be a part of the control effort. All but the crab meal from the Chesapeake Bay are techniques and practices we use here in our western PA gardens as well.

Some of you might be familiar with Alice Waters, long time gardener and chef at the famous California upscale restaurant *Chez Panisse*. She's been after the White House administration for years to put in an organic vegetable garden. Waters believes that "food should not only taste good, it should also be local, sustainable, and healthful," (sound familiar?). These important tenets of gardening are at the top of Assistant White House Chef Sam Kass' menu. Locavore might be the new buzz word used for White House kitchen staff members who had a say in what was to be grown, and where to get what couldn't.

The White House is in gardening zone 7, and I would guess that there might be a few cool season crops in the new garden by now; lettuce and spinach, peas, leeks and green onions, that is if all the beds were ready and everything went as planned. Hopefully it did because I don't like the idea of a failed first attempt at gardening by Michele Obama; she could take it out on her husband. And believe you me, you don't want the scorn of an unhappy gardener, especially if said gardener happens to be your spouse!

George Washington and Thomas Jefferson were both avid gardeners. My wife and I have visited each of their estates and have been inspired to be better gardeners by what we saw there. I like to think that the spirits of these two great gardeners visit the grounds of The White House, keeping an eye on what's being grown, and maybe, in a spiritual kind of way, offer tips on gardening, and other things.

The White House vegetable garden (2009)

Through the Seasons

*A relatively new plant pest has eased its way down into
Pennsylvania from points north. The Viburnum Leaf Beetle
devoured one of my native viburnums (Arrowwood) and will
probably do the same to more. But that shrub never acted like it
wanted to bloom anyway so I dug it up and put a nice little
Kentucky Redbud in its place. Actually, the redbud is native to
Pennsylvania too; I brought it up from Kentucky so now I call it
my Kentucky Redbud. I wonder why I don't see many redbud
trees around here.*

King Arthur's Scrubby Shrubbery

The "Knights Who Say Ni!" demanded a shrubbery from King
Arthur so that he might pass through their patch of woodland.
They required one that "looked nice" and wasn't "too expensive."
After King Arthur purchased a shrubbery from "Roger the
Shrubber" and presented it to the Knights Who Say Ni! they
demanded he bring them a second one: "Then, when you have
found the shrubbery, you must place it here, beside this
shrubbery, only slightly higher, so we get the two-level effect with
a little path running down the middle."

Some of you might recall the hilarity of the aforementioned
scene from the comedy film *Monty Python and the Holy Grail*, a
1975 movie spoofing the legends of King Arthur's quest to find
the Holy Grail (it inspired 2005's Tony Award-winning musical

Spamalot). The Knights Who Say Ni! neglected to mention which variety of shrub they'd prefer King Arthur bring them so I thought I'd offer a few suggestions for the upcoming sequel *King Arthur's Scrubby Shrubbery.*

King Arthur would be looking for easy to grow shrubs, and ones that looked nice in the landscape requiring very little maintenance. He'd surely want to consider Ilex (Holly) for those Ni! saying knights. With over 400 species to choose from, most varieties are self-sustaining once established in the garden or landscape. I trim mine to excess and every year it comes back with vigor. Which might be one setback when considering holly – if you allow it to grow freely, it'll freely grow.

Ubiquitous rhododendrons and azaleas definitely fit the bill for shrubbery that looks nice. When we first moved here, there were several large well-established rhoddys that needed un-established. You've seen them – gigantic bushy green additions to a house, which flower. I finally decided to tear out my addition several years ago and now I have a trimmed down version that I call my bonsai rhoddy. King Arthur might choose other colors besides purple flowering rhododendrons: yellow, white, orange, and pink

to name a few. There are thousands of hybrids, encompassing nearly every flower color.

I think junipers (Juniperus) would be a shrub the The Ni! saying knights would find pleasing. Also known as conifers, there's approximately 50-60 species growing in dry forest and hillsides throughout the northern hemisphere. Cultivars for the landscape, ones that would help provide "the two-level effect with a little path running down the middle," include low-growing and slow-spreading J. procumbens. Junipers tolerate a wide range of soils and conditions, and are useful for hot, sunny sites (bonus: pruning is rarely necessary).

Semi-evergreen and evergreen euonymus (Spindletree), some with gorgeous variegation, is a sure pick to please those demanding knights. Fortunei cultivars (Wintercreeper) are mound-forming and I'm sure J. 'Emerald 'n Gold' paired with the above-mentioned juniper would be perfect for "the two-level effect with a little path running down the middle." Variegated varieties need plenty of sun to enhance leaf variegation and having several 'Emerald 'n Gold' varieties along a sunny path in the front or back yard would make those knights say Ni! even louder.

I'm going to suggest shrubberys in containers for use in the sequel. That way, there'll be more space for shrubs along the paths in the Knights' patch of woodland. This knight's damsel in distress bought him a cute little arborvitae (Thuja occidentalis 'Smaragd') for his birthday that will find a new home in a pot. I'm positive it'll look very appealing and can almost guarantee that if those Knights Who Say Ni! come around here, they'll hush in wonder and amazement at my idea. Boxwoods are also good candidates for use in containers. Be sure to choose pots that match the size of your shrub, ten or twelve-inches in diameter would be good for a two or three-foot plant, and be sure they have good drainage.

For scent, lilacs (Syringa) top the list of aromatic spring flowering shrubs and Zone 5 landscapes wouldn't be the same without them, nor would the woodlands of those Ni! saying Knights. Syringa vulgaris, the common purple lilac, can be seen, and smelled, just about everywhere during spring. Some top out at over 30 feet in height, an indication of their staying power and longlivedness – lilacs adorned the landscape of early America, dating from the 1700s. Some folks say purple varieties are more fragrant so if you really want to please your knight who says Ni!, look for S. vulgaris 'Macrostachya' or 'Katherine Havermeyer.'

Since you probably won't find Roger the Shrubber available for your shrub purchasing needs, here's a few resources where you can find spring and summer flowering shrubs:

- ✓ Forest Farm – Williams, Oregon; (541) 846-7269; forestfarm.com
- ✓ Monrovia – Hahn Nursery, 5443 Babcock Blvd. Pittsburgh; (412) 635-7475
- ✓ Spring Hill Nursery – Harrison, Ohio; (513) 354-1509

Through the Seasons

Lastly, you might want to watch *Monty Python and the Holy Grail* before you get too busy foolin' with shrubbery and other landscape and garden plants.

I yanked four ugly non-native shrubs from a spot directly in front of the house and I've decided to use native shrubs or ornamental trees in their place. But I probably won't be choosing Arrowwood viburnums or Japanese maples. My wife Maureen will probably object to my decision not to use Japanese maples, but if I do all the digging shouldn't I get to decide what goes in the holes? Wishful thinking.

Through the Seasons

Through the Seasons

Out of the New, Into the Old

Most writers I know have separate full-time jobs. I'm one of those that must supplement my writing income with a part-time job. A 40-hour workweek has eluded me for the past several years and so recently I began driving a school bus. I'm finished with the morning route at 8:30, and by 9:00 I can be back home at my desk. If there are deadlines due, and they usually are, I have several hours to work on them before I have to leave for the afternoon route. This schedule has its good and bad points though. The good is the time period between 9:00 am and 2:00 pm; I can get a lot of writing done during that time. The downside to this is a little harder to explain.

Here in western PA school starts in August and ends around the first of June. Guess what? Most of that stretch of time isn't made for gardeners; it's made for plants and flowers that need a dormant period. I don't know any humans that "stop growing and conserve energy until better cultural conditions present themselves" (Marie Iannotti, About.com Gardening Guide). However, I admit that I sometimes slip into a period of inactivity after my morning bus route, especially on dreary gray cold days, when I'd rather be hibernating instead of trying to meet a deadline or write about warm season gardening.

Nonetheless, driving a school bus during the school year provides me with an opportunity to see some extraordinary pre and post-season gardens. My bus route takes me through Amish

Through the Seasons

country, and Amish country gardens are immaculate, hardly a weed can be seen, and everything looks to be in exactly the place it's supposed to be – what's out of place are the 8 Amish children that ride my bus. They attend their own school, I drop them off at an intersection and they walk a couple of miles the rest of the way. I'd love to ask them about their gardens but never do.

I wonder what those Amish children are thinking as they ride. There are a few kids who have small hand-held video game systems; Nintendo DS is a popular one. The radio is on sometimes, and most middle school and high school riders have cell phones out from time to time. I know the Amish kids see and hear all of this technological stuff, and I can only imagine what they must be thinking about it. I wonder if when they get on the bus they feel like they're leaving an old world, and entering a new one.

Looking back only a few short 20 years ago, I compare then and now and see major technology changes that have impacted the way I do things. All except for the way I garden, it's like the Amish stepping out of the old and into the new, only in reverse: When I step into the garden, I'm stepping out of the new and into the old, and I wouldn't have it any other way.

Part III - Summer

Through the Seasons

Since moving from Kentucky in 1988, I've come to love summertime in western Pennsylvania. Kentucky's heat and humidity is oppressive compared to what it is here. The Green River, a tributary of the Ohio River, runs through the small rural town of Greensburg, Kentucky. So-named because of its color and depth, the Green River also influences the amount of humidity that's always present during the summer months, humidity so thick you can walk on it.

Lazy Gardening

Overheard at a recent garden party: "I was telling him how the neighbors are saying how beautiful our flower beds are and he said, 'If they looked closer they'd see there's no mulch!' After he said that, things went downhill fast!" Maureen and I have had similar spats. Just the other day at the supper table we got into such a heated debate over some garden triviality that our teen son, AJ, told us to shut up because we sounded like two bickering teenagers. I think the heat of summer is partly to blame for a short fuse or two, that's okay though, we're allowed.

High humidity creates a short fuse – and makes me lazy; when it creeps upward I put off my garden chores until the last rays of sunlight are flickering through the trees. And even then, my chores are mostly ones that don't require hardly any physical exertion: moving an empty wheelbarrow, watering with the garden hose, picking ripe tomatoes. And Lord help you if you're around me when the mower breaks and it's 90 degrees! By the time mid-summer arrives, I'm a very lazy gardener with a short fuse, especially during the hazy humid days of August.

Having admitted my laziness and hot temper, I'll try to redeem myself with a few words for those of you who don't mind gardening when the air is thick with humidity. First, before you go rushing off into the sun, be sure your body is prepared for what awaits it; this could entail things like stretching, hydration, and applying sunscreen. (Watch what you use for hydration; beer is not recommended until after sunset.) Next, it might behoove you to wear appropriate clothing, long-sleeved shirts and pants if your skin is especially sensitive to biting bugs, and a wide-brimmed hat to help keep the noggin cool. I'm not one for wearing gloves, but by all means wear them if you think it's necessary.

When you venture out to tackle a few gardening chores during the heat of the day pace yourself, don't try to do too much at one time. And if it's possible, get out early in the morning and try to get the bulk of the tough jobs done before it gets too hot. Hot weather gardening means shade gardening for me so if there's any work in full sun, forget it (southerners refer to this as slow gardening), once the sun sets, I'm usually more energetic.

I should mention a very important health concern here: Heat exhaustion and heat stroke. Heat exhaustion is what happens when you're working outside (or inside), and excessive sweating causes a loss of body fluids, which in turn causes your body to overheat. Heat stroke is a life-threatening medical condition brought on by a complete shutdown of your internal cooling system causing brain damage or damage to other internal organs.

You may not even be aware you're suffering from heat exhaustion if you aren't paying attention to what your body is telling you, so if you're sweating, you need to be drinking plenty of fluids to replace what's being lost. Symptoms of heat exhaustion include profuse sweating and pale skin that's moist and cool, muscle cramps or pains may occur and you might feel faint or dizzy. Heat stroke symptoms: unconscious or abnormal mental state (dizziness, confusion, or hallucinations); flushed, hot, and dry skin, elevated blood pressure, or a person could hyperventilate. If you're not sure what's wrong, or don't know what to do, call a doctor; however, if heat stroke is suspected call 911, or if possible take the person to the hospital emergency room immediately.

Through the Seasons

I don't want to alarm or scare anyone into not getting out and enjoying the summer weather, but being a lazy gardener will practically eliminate your chances of getting heat exhaustion and heat stroke. Of course, my laziness might be more or less strenuous than yours.

I've heard it said that age plays tricks on you. But it's no joke that as I've aged I've become much more of a slow gardener, especially during the heat of the summer gardening season. The perfect summer day would be one where the air is almost as cool as a mountain spring, sunshine is softened behind high cirrus clouds (Mother calls them fair weather clouds), and I'm relaxing in the garden, watching a caterpillar munching on a leaf. And not minding that it's the leaf of a favorite flower.

Through the Seasons

I like to include a couple of articles about lawns in my column over the course of the summer. Although I sometimes think lawns can be boring to write about, I think they've had a huge influence on gardening. I can't remember a time during my childhood that we didn't have a yard to play in. One yard in particular comes to mind, grass in it was sparse, and it was mostly dirt and crushed cinder, I never went barefoot in that yard, but Mother did. She always told us kids to take care of our feet, but I never understood why until I reached adulthood and had a yard of my own. It's because grassy yards are made for bare feet, and if you take care of your feet they just might become tough enough to walk on any type of yard.

Lawn Love

It'd probably be safe to say that avid gardeners don't give much thought to mowing the lawn. It's a chore most would consider rather boring, especially if you have a big yard, and I've done my fair share of complaining about it for years. Most of my attention during the growing season is on the vegetable garden, potted and hanging annuals, and perennials, usually in that order. However, grass is the most carefree plants in our landscape and we shouldn't complain about mowing.

After all, our grass doesn't complain, even during dry spells.
Containers with annuals couldn't last without careful attention to watering, and a vegetable garden wouldn't be very productive unless moisture content in the surrounding soil was adequate for strong root development. I think lawns give you much more than you give them, all things considered.

It wasn't until after the invention of "mowing machines" in 1830 that folks started worrying about having a proper lawn. Before then, scythes and grazing animals took care of high growing grasses, and lawns were actually pastures. Back in the day, when someone spoke of their "lawn," they were referring to a stretch of open, grass-covered land – a pasture. And then along came the Elizabethan times, when uppity English men and women created manicured lawns for their spoiled kids to run and play on. Shakespeare once said "A lawn of luscious green, shall make thy children manly mean." (He didn't really say that, but could've.)

Through the Seasons

The influence of the English on American gardening (and yardening) reached a peak during the Victorian Era (1837-1901) when folks in the U.S. began to build large and elaborate houses that reflected their position in society. Lawns became prominent landscape features, and having one that was well manicured and cared for was an important status symbol. This, of course, led to present day lawn love, which isn't a bad thing. Unless...

Watering. Yes, watering the lawn might be the biggest detriment to having one. I have almost three acres of lawn. With such a huge yard, it's impossible for me to water during dry spells. But I don't worry about it, because if Nature doesn't provide the moisture, lawns have a built-in slow growth mechanism that causes them to go dormant until the next rain. Those of you with smaller lawns who might want to water between dry periods should follow these recommendations:

✓ Water only when your grass needs it. When your grass is thirsty, it'll take on a blue-gray tint, and if you notice footprints staying on the grass longer than usual, it's time to water.

Through the Seasons

✓ Water an inch a week as a rule of thumb. Here's how to tell. Set out several same-diameter cans with an inch mark on each. Spread the cans around where you'll be watering and time how long it takes for your sprinklers to fill the cans to the 1-inch mark. Water for that length of time.

✓ Water early in the morning. Some water evaporates before it hits the ground. You'd be surprised how much evaporation occurs on a hot, windy day. Watering between 4 AM and 9 AM is best, the air is cool and wind is usually calm.

✓ If you've laid new sod, or recently reseeded, watering will be more important and you'll do it more frequently to help roots get established. And always use good straw mulch after reseeding and watering a new area.

If you have toddlers and a yard full of clover there's a good chance that one of these days your barefoot little girl or boy will step on a honeybee. Although bee stings are painful, and in some cases quite serious, seeing bees buzzing around your yard and garden is a good sign. It means that you're probably not using harmful chemicals and the bees feel safe collecting pollen from the flowers and plants in your landscape. And as Martha Stewart says, "that's a good thing."

Through the Seasons

In Greek mythology Artemis was the daughter of Zeus and goddess of the hunt, wild animals, the wilderness and a couple of other things. Some botanists say the fragrant herb Artemisia annua was named after Artemis, but I can't find any reference to that fact. However, I can always find sweet Annie growing in my wife's herb garden. There's only one other herb besides sweet Annie with a fragrance I'd love to see bottled for men – lavender.

Herbs and Pawpaws

Mmmm, the sweet aroma of sweet Annie greets me as I make my way through the garage and reluctantly climb on the mower. Facing the ever-dreaded chore of mowing is made somewhat easier to bear, if only for a few short minutes, by the odor of a most wonderful herb. Soon, it's the odor and noise of a small combustible engine that fills my nostrils and ears. As I begin the monotonous chore, I know it won't be long before the mower deck is removed and the snowplow blade is reinstalled.

Maureen's bustling about in the herb garden, snipping this herb and that one as if prodded by some unseen herbal goddess, this is a sure sign that it's harvest time for herbalists. One of her favorites, and one of mine, is sweet Annie (Artemisia annua) an annual that can reach heights of up to six feet. Its value to herbalists is its ability when dried to retain its sweet aroma, making it highly prized in homemade wreaths.

Through the Seasons

Known for its wonderful fragrance instead of its inconspicuous blossoms, Sweet Annie needs a sunny spot with lots of room. Plants should be spaced 2½-3 feet apart. If established in the garden, and allowed to go to seed, some plants will self-sow. Maureen also buys plants in spring for added insurance that she'll have plenty for wreath making. Cut long stems when little yellow seed heads form, tie in bundles and hang in a dry place. If you need hanging space, I'll be glad to put up another sweet Annie drying line in my garage.

Speaking of sweetness, Julia Larson of Grove City sent one of her heirloom tomatoes home with Maureen a couple of weeks ago. 'Potato Top' came from seeds Julia received in the mail from Doug Oster. Oster's gardening column, *The Backyard Gardener*, appears in the Pittsburgh Post-Gazette and he sponsors the "'Potato Top' Tomato Project." For more information and a possible free sampling of 'Potato Top' seeds, email Oster at doster@post-gazette.com, or call 412-263-1484.

Spreading even more sweetness, Frank Baker stopped in the other evening with fruit from one of his many Pawpaw trees (*Asimina triolba*). I didn't know Kentucky banana trees grew this far north. Yellow, sweet, and custardy pawpaws don't look

Through the Seasons

anything like a banana, but their taste comes close. It's a mix of mango, banana and pineapple. Frank tells me they make preserves from the fruit. The poor man's banana, a pawpaw provides three times as much vitamin C as an apple and contains all essential amino acids, making it a fruit worth its weight in, well, bananas. Gardening is one sweet hobby!

Pawpaws are known as Kentucky bananas in the Bluegrass State. I'm not sure why, I'm a native Kentuckian and have tasted pawpaws and don't think they taste anything like a banana. As a matter of fact, I wouldn't recommend pawpaws be eaten at all, unless you're lost in the wilderness, starving, and happen upon a pawpaw tree bearing ripe fruit. But subjective opinions are a dime a dozen, especially ones that deal with taste buds. We all know a good aroma when we sniff it, unlike the uniqueness of our taste buds, our noses seem alike and what smells pleasant to me will usually smell that way to others. Sniffing Artemisia or tasting Kentucky bananas are two separate things gardeners might do, but of those two things, I can only recommend sniffing Artemisia.

Through the Seasons

There are things a gardener does in each season that makes use of what she's learnt in previous seasons. Planting things that you won't see bloom until a future point in time is one of them. For example, if you planted a certain flower that only blooms in spring, and it has done well over the course of several seasons, it's probably a good flower to use again. Experience is a great teacher, just ask a gardener.

Bulbs, Tubers, Corms and Rhizomes

Is it already time to start thinking about planting spring flowering bulbs? It seems like I just started wearing flip flops and now fall catalogs are arriving in the mail prompting me to put my digging shoes back on. Geesh! What happened to the long hazy lazy days of summer? It makes you wonder if time really does fly, regardless if you're having fun or not. But planting fall bulbs can be fun and I've a new spot I'll be utilizing for just that purpose. So, why don't y'all find a spot for a new flowerbed and join me in planting a few of your favorites?

If you were to ask me what time of year I like best my answer would be: Spring, summer, fall, and I'd have to reluctantly include winter. Each season has its own attractions for each of us. I've heard folks say they would rather it stay warm year-round, others tell of their wishes for the constant coolness of autumn, and wouldn't spring be nice 365 days a year – imagine not ever

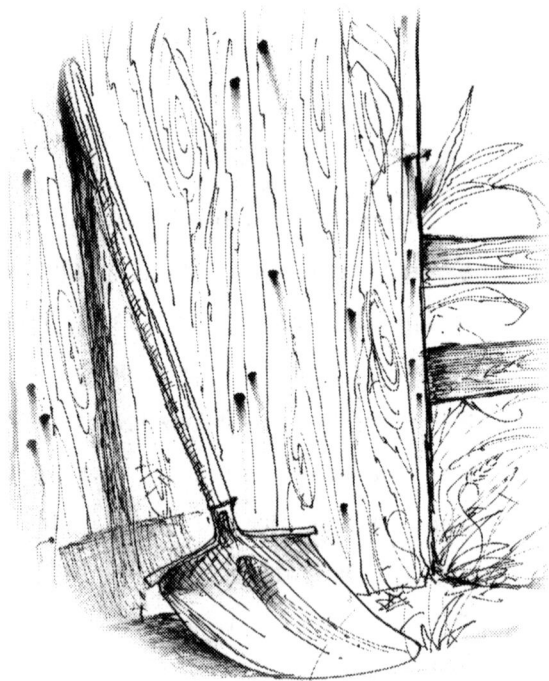

having to worry about replacing dead or dying plants. For some, winter might be the preferred season, we all have an affinity for gift giving in December that I wish could last year round.

But perhaps it's the harvest season that might rank highest for a veggie gardener or farmer. Our tomatoes have ripened, with more still to come (I grow all heirlooms), and Maureen is picking peppers: Banana, Cayenne, and Hungarian. Our zucchini, cucumbers, and eggplant didn't survive an attack by cucumber beetles. But that's okay, we have kind-hearted neighbors who're having a bumper crop of zucchini, and I don't mind going without cukes and egg plant for a season. And then there are the farmers' markets, most within easy driving distance.

The harvest season is also the time to consider which spring flowering bulbs you're going to plant. You've already ordered, and maybe even received your bulbs by now. I order mine through Brent and Becky's Bulbs, their selections always perform well here in Zone 5. And they also send a free bulb-planting guide with each order. If you're just starting out with bulbs, the next few paragraphs will help you become a better bulber (writers sometimes take liberty and invent new words: Bulber – use as adjective or noun).

What is a bulb anyway? Put simply, a bulb is nothing more than a ball of stored energy for making a flower. Bulbs contain white meaty scales that surround and protect a flower bud in the center. The scales provide energy to the growing flower bud once it's planted. At the bottom of the bulb is a modified stem (basal plate) where roots develop. Spring flowering bulbs require a period of cold before they can flower; this means they must be planted in fall, about six weeks before the ground freezes.

Tubers, corms, and rhizomes are sometimes called bulbs but are not true bulbs as I have described above. Crocuses and gladiolus are two examples of flowers grown from corms. Dahlias are considered tuberous, and lily-of-the-valley is grown from rhizomes. Narcissus, tulips, and hyacinth are three examples of true bulbs that flower in spring. If you want to tell the difference, remember that true bulbs have fleshy scales attached to a basal plate (daffodils), corms are swollen stem bases (crocus and cyclamen), tubers are uneven swollen stems or roots (dahlias) and rhizomes are horizontal swollen stems (lily-of-the-valley and cannas).

From now on, whenever you hear me talk of bulbs, take into consideration that I'm also referring to corms, tubers, and rhizomes unless I state otherwise.

Spring flowering bulbs require a sustained period of cold temperature in order for them to produce their flowers. They survive underground by living off the energy stored in their bulbous root systems. When you see daffs, tulips, and other spring flowering perennials dying back to the ground, they're not really dying, they're just going dormant until their next flowering period the following year.

Once you've decided on a spot for your spring flowering bulbs, prepare the site in mid to late summer. Now would be an ideal time to do this, but don't wear flip-flops when using a shovel (believe me, it's hazardous to your feet). Most bulbs like an area that receives full sun and has well-drained soil. I always recommend working in composted manure, or mushroom compost; if the soil in the new spot seems a little heavy and wet, add coarse sand and lots of organic matter.

You can purchase tools made specifically for planting bulbs that make it a little easier, but a hand trowel or small shovel will work. Bulbs should be planted at a depth four or five times its size. For example, if you have a three-inch bulb you'll plant it 12 or 15 inches deep. Plant bulbs en masse if you're looking to fill in a bank or hillside, or if you want to naturalize a large area of your lawn. Bulbs can also be forced into blooming indoors, but that's a topic for another article. After you've planted your bulbs, mulch with a layer of straw, pine needles, or shredded leaves.

Bulbs to consider for spring (deer resistant):

- ✓ Alliums – these members of the Liliaceae family of plants are also known as ornamental onions. Some are large and bold ('Globemaster') while others are small and inconspicuous (karataviense). Most have globe-shaped flowers that come in a variety of colors.

✓ Fritillaria – with their downward facing blooms create a stunning and interesting display. Imperialis is most common and has yellow, orange-red, or red flowers. F. 'Rubra' is a beautiful deep vermilion red.

✓ Chionodoxa – Glory-of-the-snow is glorious indeed with its racemes of star-shaped flowers shining in early spring. 'Pink Giant' is no giant, only growing 4 to 5 inches tall with pink flowers.

Daffodils, tulips, crocuses, and lots of other spring flowering bulbs come in a wide variety of shapes, shades, and sizes and you shouldn't have any problems finding a combination that just might cause spring to become your favorite season of the year.

Some bulbers go to the extreme for their spring flower show. I've seen photographs in <u>Martha Stewart Living</u> of some of her extreme plantings of daffs, crocus, and other spring bloomers. Immense sections of her immaculately manicured landscape carpeted in yellows, pinks and purples are stunning to look at. But for some reason I just can't picture Martha planting all those bulbs. I reckon she did though, she does everything else.

Through the Seasons

Hardiness zone maps shouldn't confuse you. I live in Zone 5. Or is it 5a? No, I think it's changed to 5b, or maybe it's Zone 6? Didn't I just say that zone maps shouldn't be confusing? Oh well, perhaps the following article will help clear things up a bit.

In the Zone

Whenever I visit my family in Kentucky, it's inevitable that I'll compare my garden to theirs. I had the chance to do just that a couple of weeks ago and one of the conversations concerning vegetables went something like this:

Me: "You're eating tomatoes already? Mine won't be ready for a couple more weeks."

Chuck (my brother, biting into one of his just-picked): "Oh really? Too bad."

Me (excitedly): "But we had zucchini and cukes ready almost a month ago!"

"Oh." Chuck replies nonchalantly.

And so it goes, a zone 5 gardener wanting zone 6 gardening.

I'm sure you've often thought about what it might be like to garden in a warmer zone. Chuck doesn't worry about digging up cannas or four 'o clocks as I do, he spreads a layer of mulch over them at summer's end and they're good to go till bloom time next year. I tried leaving four 'o clocks in over the winter here; mulched them with at least a six-inch layer of straw and they barely made a showing the next year.

Through the Seasons

There are at least three different hardiness zone maps: the United States Department of Agriculture (USDA) has a 1990 version, the American Horticultural Society (AHS) has their plant heat zone map, and the National Arbor Day Foundation's hardiness zone map. The USDA is in the process of updating their map "using new mapping technology and an extended set of meteorological data." There's been some debate about which of these maps gardeners should use, but I don't think it matters in the long run. I think of my garden as a trial garden anyway and will sometimes plant something that is not recommended for my zone just to see if it matters to the plant. I'm sure you do the same.

Finding your hardiness zone, or growing zone as they're sometimes called, is accomplished by viewing a color coded map and seeing where the area you live falls within subdivided color coded sections or zones. Most of these maps are viewable on the Web with tools you can use to help you find your zone. (Visit www.arborday.org/media/zones.cfm to see the National Arbor Day Foundation's newest 2006 hardiness zone map).

The USDA hardiness zone map divides North America into 11 hardiness zones. Zone 1 is the coldest and zone 11 is the warmest. These zones are based on ten-degree F. differences in the average annual minimum temperatures. Each zone is divided into A and B regions based on five-degree differences. Using

Through the Seasons

these zones as guidelines helps us decide which plants will perform best in our gardens. A good rule of thumb is to choose plants that will be more cold-tolerant rather than less. For example, if a zone 5b site borders a zone 6a, search first for zone 5b plants, then zone 6a plants. (If the A and B divisions confuse you, there's no rule that says you have to use them.)

According to an article by Peter Del Tredici (*The New USDA Plant Hardiness Map*) the first hardiness zone map was "published in 1927 in Alfred Rehder's ground-breaking *Manual of Cultivated Trees and Shrubs.*" Mr. Rehder, it seems, had his own idea of 8 zones instead of the more modern 11 and assigned all the plants listed in his Manual to one of the 8 zones. Del Tredici states that this map "stood alone until 1938" at which time Donald Wyman drew up another hardiness zone map using data from a U.S. Weather Bureau map. Mr. Wyman's map was updated in 1951, 1967, and again in 1971. In 1960 the USDA began questioning the uniformity of Wyman's map and produced their own updated version.

Of course we all know other factors come into play besides hardiness zones when it comes to a plant's ability to grow and thrive in the garden. Alfred Rehder pointed out some of these factors in his 1927 Manual: "There are, however, many other factors besides temperature in winter which will influence the hardiness and growth of certain plants, as soil, its physical as well as chemical composition, exposure, rainfall, humidity of the air, shelter from the cold winds."

Microclimates are another consideration. Sometimes the climate of a small area such as an urban community or the area surrounding houses can allow some plants not normally hardy in a certain colder zone to live and grow as though they were in a warmer zone. Perhaps I should try a few of Chuck's zone 6 plants in such areas around my house – the beautiful crepe myrtle comes immediately to mind.

And don't forget about the "grandparent factor" either. Plants your grandparents grow in their gardens are ones you should seriously consider growing in your garden (if you live in the same zone). Plants native to your zone should be given top priority; they have already proven their stability.

If you have family living in another state compare their hardiness zone to yours and if there's only a zone or two difference, try a plant rated for their zone in yours. You just might be surprised to find a plant that's rated for a warmer zone will actually live, grow, and thrive in a colder one. Trial gardening is what I call it.

Along with the hardiness zone map, there's also a heat zone map that tells you the average number of days it gets above 86 degrees in your area. It's a colorful map with darks indicating cooler zones and lighter shades indicating warmer ones. The map shows me that my area in western Pennsylvania has greater than seven, but less than 30 days, on average, of temperatures above the 86 degree threshold. Kentucky has greater than 60, but less than 90 days of 86 degree days. I'm jealous!

Through the Seasons

Dirt or Soil?

Is dirt soil, or is soil dirt? What's the difference in meaning? When I was a kid Mother would yell at me after coming in from playing in the dirt, I used to get beads of dirt in the cracks of skin under my neck. Mother would say, "Now look at you! You've got grandma's black beads under your neck! Get in the bathroom and wash your face and hands right this minute! And don't forget grandma's black beads!" I don't remember seeing Grandma wearing a black beaded necklace.

I loved walking barefoot in dirt when I was a kid. I remember how little puffs of dirt-smoke would rise in slow motion out from under my feet when I stomped in it, and how cool I thought it looked. It reminded me of watching Neil Armstrong's moon walk, and how moon-dirt dust rose from beneath his boot as he walked on the

surface. One of my cousins used to eat dirt; I tried it only after she said it was some kind of pie.

What I don't understand is why some folks prefer to use the word soil instead of saying dirt. Soil reminds me of something little Johnny does: "Now look at you, and phew wee! You've done went and soiled your diaper!" Pet owners say things like "Oh my, it looks like Fido has soiled the carpet again!"

If you're a gardener and you're digging, what's that substance your digging, soil or dirt? There are 13 entries for soil at *Dictionary.com* and 7 for dirt (that's strange, two odd numbers for amounts, and these numbers are my lucky ones, but I digress). Here's one definition for soil: "The top layer of the earth's surface consisting of rock and mineral particles mixed with organic matter." Here's one for dirt: "The part of the earth's surface consisting of humus and disintegrated rock.

Humus and organic matter are included in both definitions and these two substances are considered to be black gold to gardeners. This tells me that dirt and soil is more or less the same thing. Thank goodness I've cleared this up for everybody, well, almost everybody. master gardeners (myself included) and hortheads enjoy using the word soil instead of dirt at garden lectures, so don't ever tell them you're planting in dirt, say soil, it's what they like to hear.

Part IV - Fall

Through the Seasons

Two words uttered never sounded so, well, final, as "The End." I used to tease my kids when they were little by telling them a story, a very short story: "Once upon a time, the end." The end of the gardening season for folks living in the temperate zone is usually around October, harvesting is winding down and we're preparing the gardens for their dormant period – also known as closing the garden. Pulling spent stalks, stems, and shoots isn't an appealing job, but gardening has to end, and start, somewhere. In all actuality, gardening never really ends anyway; the garden is always evolving, which if you think about it, makes the gardener immortal, philosophically speaking.

Clean it Up

Last week I wrote about a special method I use to close the garden – my "do nothing" method allows me to leave some spent plant material in the garden to decompose over the winter. I explained that it might help lessen the aches and pains caused by the normal method one might use to close the garden (cutting, removing, loading and hauling). I hope my method doesn't come across as a lazy man's way out of doing end-of-season chores, because it's not; there are lots of other chores to do that require a certain amount of elbow grease.

Through the Seasons

There are four shovels, three rakes, several hoes, and a bucket full of other hand-held digging, weeding, and planting tools in my garage. Each of these will need cleaned before I store them in the shed. First, it's hand-held pruners and trimmers that are taken apart, cleaned with a dry cloth and then oiled. I use what most gardeners consider to be the Cadillac of all hand-held pruners – Felco (around 40 bucks, well spent). And I use only Felco pruners because they have more than proven their worth in the garden. Please, don't buy cheap pruning shears; it's like tossing your hard-earned dollars onto the compost heap.

If cutting seems to take more effort, re-sharpen your pruners. Hold the pruners in your left hand (for right handers) and sharpen the blade using a light or medium grade ceramic sharpening stone held at a 20-degree angle. Turn the pruners over and use the stone at a 5-degree angle to remove any burring from the blade. Sharpening your pruners now will save you a little time next spring, and you won't have to worry about dull pruners when cutting spring flowers for those first bouquets of the season.

Through the Seasons

Shovels, garden trowels, hand-held weeding tools, and other small tools you use for planting can be easily cleaned with warm soapy water and a scrub brush. That is if you haven't neglected them all summer and are now faced with scraping off hard-as-cement caked on mud and dirt. (Why haven't they invented a garden trowel that dirt won't stick to?) After cleaning, use medium grit sandpaper to remove any rust that may have developed over the season and then oil the metal blade with lightweight household oil such as 3-In-One or WD-40. I've heard that some folks push their shovels and trowels in a gritty sand/oil mix and store them there over the winter. Why not?

Lawn mowers, grass and hedge trimmers, and loppers should be cleaned as well. Removing grass and dirt from your lawn care equipment will help keep them in top shape for years to come. My old Wheel Horse 12 has served me well for over 15 years and I attribute its longevity to proper maintenance at the end, and at the start, of the mowing season. Undersides of mowers should be cleaned and then coated with a thick layer of all-purpose grease before being stored. Grass trimmers should be hosed and allowed to dry, and treat loppers as

Through the Seasons

you would pruners. Also remember to drain all gas from power equipment and store or dispose of properly.

It's hard to imagine cleaning and storing tools and mowers, and closing the garden when the temperature outside is a balmy 85 degrees. The past week or two has been more like August, not October. The weather forecast say's it'll be much cooler by the time you read this, and perhaps then we'll all start realizing it's the end of another most enjoyable gardening season.

Closing the garden sounds too final. I don't like calling it that. I just do what needs to be done when stuff has finished growing. My gardening activity in fall is mainly determined by the weather. I don't usually try to protect flowering plants when the first frost rolls in, and I'm not upset by that decision. I let Nature take care of the garden for the most part, and it's not really closed, it's just taking a long nap.

Through the Seasons

Presidential elections can be exciting and 2009 brought a rather entertaining and historical election. Youth, old age, beauty, and race all played a part in what led to the election of the first African-American President – Barrack Obama. And once he moved into the White House, his wife Michelle proceeded to announce plans for a new garden! Running against the President was Senator John McCain, representing the Republican Party, and probably most of the cotton top generation as well. His VP running mate, and then Governor of Alaska, Sarah Palin, appealed to millions of men. The Republicans lost the election, but I think all the gardeners in that party were consoled by the fact that Mrs. Obama broke ground for a new garden!

Politically Correct Gardening

With all the attention Joe the Plumber and Joe Six-pack have been getting recently and the presidential election less than a week from now, I thought it only fair to give Joe the Gardener an opportunity to speak. I decided to ask him which presidential candidate would have the best White House garden, and why. The following interview is not the truth, is nowhere near the whole truth, and is nothing but fiction. However, should you feel inclined to change who you're voting for in the upcoming presidential election based on what you read in this interview, do so only after serious consideration as to which plant(s) your candidate might have in his or her garden, and if those plants might be suitable companion plants to those you grow in your garden.

I interviewed Joe the Gardener on a chilly October day in his backyard garden. Joe's garden is much like yours or mine, and he gave me a quick tour before we sat down for the interview. Explaining that his garden wasn't much to look at now, Joe said he was ready for someone to show him a new approach to gardening, and that he was tired of seeing the same old tough-as-nails plants and wondered if a few tender-as-a-kitten ones would add a softer, more feminine feel to his garden. Joe's Sweet Annie, much of it frost-bitten, seemed to acknowledge his words with movement, or so I thought (it was a calm day, and there was no wind).

<u>The Interview</u>

The Write Gardener: Who do you think is the better gardener, Senator Obama or Senator McCain?

Joe the Gardener: Well, since you don't hear or see anything about the gardening habits of either candidate in the news, I'll take a wild guess and say Senator Obama.

WG: What makes you think Senator Obama would be a better gardener?

JG: He looks more refined. And of course it's easy to see the age difference. I think there are a lot of things a young gardener can accomplish that a much older gardener would never attempt. Could you see Senator McCain tackling the job of pruning an overgrown shrub, or digging the planting hole for a tree?

WG: Some might consider that an ageist statement.

JG: Oh? I'm sorry. I don't mean to be stereotyping, or offensive. I'm just saying that the older you get, the less you can do, in the garden anyway. Look at me, I'm 55-years old and I get sore muscles from just looking at a pair of pruners. You know how long it takes me to dig a hole a foot deep?

WG: Uh, no. How long?

JG: Depends on what year it is and if the ground is wet.

WG: What type of garden do you think each candidate might have?

JG: I'd say Obama might have more of a formal garden, with symmetry, some topiary and stone urns, and lots of tall stately plants like lilies. McCain's garden would be much less formal I think, a cottage garden with Joe-pye weed and purple cone flowers and possibly a tire planter or two filled with summer annuals like zinnias and marigolds.

Through the Seasons

WG: Do you think it's important for the next President to practice composting?

JG: I don't think either one of them know what it means, do they?

WG: Will Senator McCain's running mate influence your decision to choose the candidate who might have the best White House garden?

JG: Of course she will! Didn't I tell you that I'm a member of "Dudes for Palin?"

After discovering that Joe the Gardener was a member of *Dudes for Palin*, I had to end the interview for obvious reasons. I should have guessed his involvement when he said he wanted a more feminine feel to his garden.

Back to reality...

I think the White House needs a greenhouse, and our new President should be a gardener, his job is mighty stressful and we all know gardening reduces stress.

In 2009 the 1500 square feet White House garden produced 1,000 pounds of produce; in 2010 it produced 1600 pounds. As the years pass will the White House garden always be as productive? I hope so and wish the same for what's being discussed inside as well!

Through the Seasons

Does technology have a place in the garden? I've often wondered where it might fit in. What flower bed, back or front border? Will it need more than its fair share of water and sunlight? Will it grow well alongside roses or should it have a place all to itself? Worse yet, might it even become invasive?

Techno-gardening

The recipe for indoor gardening usually includes three simple ingredients: plant, container, and soil. Sunshine, of course, is also a necessary ingredient, available to your indoor plants, via a south-facing window or patio door. The amount of energy plants receive from sunshine is not something we as gardeners can control. The other ingredients are ones we can manipulate. We can choose from a wide variety of houseplants, most of which are considered to be tropical in one form or another. The selections of pots and containers are myriad and seem endless, and potting soils are readily available at garden centers and box stores everywhere.

Remove any one of the ingredients and it's doubtful houseplants will survive, unless they're very special. For example, tillandsia, or air plant, doesn't need soil. A member of the Bromeliad family, tillandsias will grow just about anywhere given the proper attention, or not. Attach one to a rock or seashell, on pottery or wood using glue, fishing line, or twisty ties and leave it be. It'll grow with minimal attention from you. Some wildflowers appear special. Last summer I happened upon a wild aster on the shoulder of the highway which seemed to be growing in nothing but pavement. A closer look revealed a crack where enough soil had accumulated for the roots to take hold. There are many more special plants (orchids come to mind) that grow and thrive in the wild by using host plants or some other object as their pot or container.

Traditionally, houseplants grow in potting soil in colorful containers of all shapes and sizes. Some indoor gardeners have what appear to be mini-jungles in their living rooms and dens. Tall, short, leafy, thorny, bushy, frilly plants line walls and windowsills, hang from ceilings and ledges, giving gardeners their much needed green fix during the winter months when the only thing growing outside are snowdrifts. Soon, I'll be bringing my porch plants back inside, in preparation for the winter season. Containers will once again be part of our living room furniture.

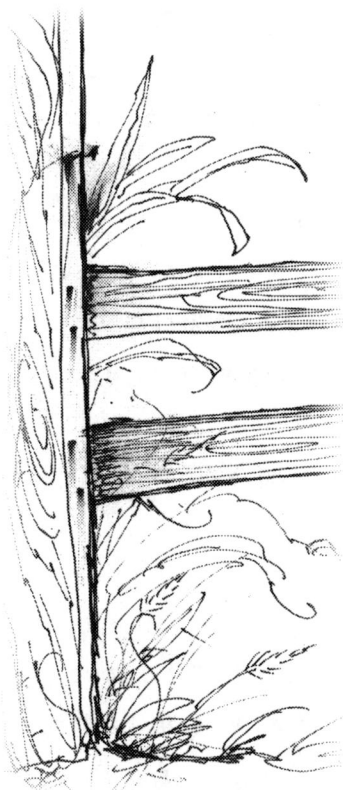

But things change, technology sees to that. Enter: AeroGrow, a company that makes and sells "indoor gardening appliances." And just what is an indoor gardening appliance? First you need to know the definition of aeroponics. Wikipedia defines it: "Aeroponics – the process of growing plants in an air or mist environment without the use of soil or an aggregate medium." AeroGrow's founder, Michael Bissonnette, came up with the idea in 2004 and engineered a unique "appliance" that you can use to grow plants "in water, nutrients, and air," no soil or pot needed.

The seed-starting gardener looking for a compact growlight unit will find AeroGrow's indoor gardening appliances quite appealing. But I think these appliances would also add an element of indoor gardening modernization that is lacking in most homes. AeroGrow's Web catalog (http://tinyurl.com/bjef43) offers an enticing selection of AeroGardens that I find quite attractive.

We all know gardening is sometimes a subjective pursuit and some of you might see this new "gardening appliance" as a bit too modern, and that's okay. As for me, I'm a huge Star Trek fan, and during a recent episode I think I saw an AeroGarden on the Enterprise. Beam me up Scotty!

I started using an iPhone about a year ago, and will probably upgrade to the latest version as soon as it's available. Iphones, and other smart phones, have applications (apps) that can help make your life a little easier. There's shopping apps, music apps, social networking apps, and yes, gardening apps. But I've yet to find an app that makes weeding and digging any easier!

Through the Seasons

I'm pretty sure I've never written an article about botany, although I couldn't really be a gardener without knowing a little bit about it, and neither could you. Consider the following piece a short condensed lesson, that's about all I can take anyway.

Botanically Speaking

It snowed yesterday. And although it didn't stick around long enough to support the life of a snowman, it could possibly serve as a foreshadowing of the woolly worm's prediction for winter: a harsh start, mild middle, and harsh ending. This may or may not hold true depending on whether or not the woolly worm you saw was colored the same as the one I saw. The early snow might suggest some measure of reliability for insect weather forecasters, but I'm not suggesting you quit watching that cutie Julie Bologna on Channel 11 at 5:00.

Woolly worms, aka woolly bears, black-ended bears, and the approved Entomological Society of America common name – Banded woolly bear, are actually the larval stage of the Isabella tiger moth. Woolly worm caterpillars feed on leaves and if they're out in force (I rarely see more than one or two here) may cause damage to ornamentals. Banded woolly bears hibernate into a deep freeze through winter, wake up in spring long enough to spin their cocoon and emerge as adult moths with yellowish-brown wings and black spots. (I've always thought that metamorphosis thing was really cool.)

There's another type of metamorphosis that you're probably not familiar with. Have you ever wondered about a flower's ultimate goal: Seeds. Flowers are the reproductive part of most plants and the many shapes, sizes, colors, aromas and varying degrees of all of these are created and designed in such a way as to attract a pollinator. Although you probably don't think about it, and I don't either because I'm too busy admiring the gorgeous blooms, seeds are the ultimate goal of many flowering plants. Simply put, seeds contain new plants. And without new plants, a gardener's garden ain't much to look at. So, from flower to seed; seed to flower – a type of metamorphosis.

Flowers contain pollen and tiny eggs called ovules. After pollination and fertilization, ovules develop into fruit which provides a covering for seeds. Some fruits are fleshy like an apple, or hard like a nut. At season's end, and once flowering is done and fruits, nuts, and berries are harvested, seeds are usually ignored (unless you're into seed saving or exchanging). I urge you to take a closer look at some of the seed heads and seed pods produced by common garden variety flowers, you might think you're looking at something from another planet.

Here's a list of several flowers with very interesting seed heads. If you're already growing these in your garden but haven't noticed their "metamorphosis," pay more attention.

- ✓ Crocosmia – this perennial is cool enough to begin with, I've mentioned it in past articles. Seeds are enclosed in pods that dry and then open, the pods look like the open mouth of the plant monster in the movie "Little Shop of Horrors" ("Feed me Seymour!").
- ✓ Echanecea – seed heads on purple coneflowers are strikingly odd in comparison to their showy flowers. Spikes and needles are a part of this cone-shaped seed head; definitely one of the most alien looking.
- ✓ Gaillardia – once blanket flower ceases petal production, its almost perfectly sphere-shaped seed head is quite beautiful. Tiny, prickly, red-orange shuttlecocks (seeds) are packed tightly together into a gorgeous little sphere.
- ✓ Rudbeckia – the "black eye" of black-eyed Susan is actually the seed head and once flowering is complete on this indigenous North American coneflower, nothing remains of the flower except its lone "black eye."
- ✓ Dandelion – this yellow yard flower's puffy and cottony seedhead is a common site all across America, and who

hasn't bent to pluck one or two for an attempt at blowing all the seeds off?

I've listed only five of perhaps hundreds of flowers that have interesting seed heads. If you have or know of a flower that produces unusually odd seed pods or seed heads, send me an email and tell me about it. I'm always looking for something new and different for my garden. Now get out there and take a closer look at some of the seed heads in your garden, before more snow arrives and covers them.

I've heard it said that the only constant is change. And my garden is constantly changing, a metamorphosis from one year to the next. I think that's largely why gardeners garden. It wouldn't be any fun if it became stagnant. The only thing I'd change if it were possible would be to somehow make all weeds as pretty as the rest of the flowers in my garden. Then I'd retire, open a weedy greenhouse and make millions selling them to y'all!

Through the Seasons

I bet you didn't know that chrysanthemums were declared queen of the fall garden. It's easy to understand why considering they're everywhere you look once chilly weather arrives in fall. I consider them less than stately, undeserving of their queenly status during fall. There are other more deserving flowers for fall – roses! End of discussion.

Falling for Mums

Fall officially began yesterday at 5:18 pm EDT. And that means chrysanthemums will start showing up everywhere. How did these showy members of the aster family become one of the most recognizable signs of autumn? I suspect it had something to do with plant propagators and the need for color in the fall garden.

Mums date back to the 15th Century when China first cultivated them as flowering herbs. The roots were thought to be a cure for headaches, and leaves were used in salads and brewed in teas. The Chinese so honored the chrysanthemum that they named a city after the flower – Chu-Hsien, which translates "Chrysanthemum City."

Sometime around 1753, Carl Linnaeus caught wind of the plant and took it upon himself to assign the botanical name "chrysanthemum." He combined the Greek words "chrysos," meaning gold colored and "anthemom" which means flowered. Gold must've been the predominant color of mums back in the day, now you see mums in various shades of magenta, yellow, orange, pink, red, and white.

In order for mums to be hardy here in our zone (5 or 6 depending on who you ask) they should have stolons. Stolons are shoots that bend to the ground or that grow horizontally above the ground and produce roots and shoots at the nodes.

Seasonal mums for fall display gardens do not usually have stolons because most are short term decorative plants that are discarded once the first hard frost hits. However, some non-hardy mums might overwinter here if in a microclimate (close to the house, protected from the elements, and heavily mulched).

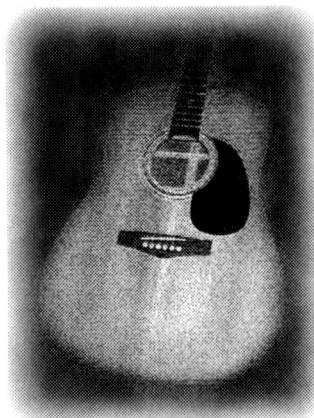

The National Chrysanthemum Society states on their Web site: "Since the chrysanthemum was first introduced into the United States during colonial times, its popularity has grown such that mums now reign as undisputed 'Queen of the Fall Flowers.' " Using mums in fall displays is easy. We leave the plants in the pots they came in and set them down inside containers that used to hold our summer annuals.

Through the Seasons

Another item used in conjunction with mums is pumpkins and gourds. We've got both growing here but the gourds aren't quite ready to pick just yet so we're using pumpkins in our fall displays. Bales of straw or hay, dried cornstalks and spent sunflower stalks are also good to use. Farmers that live close to you will usually allow you to cut a few dried corn stalks if you ask nicely. Tied together and propped on the straw bale, surrounded by pumpkins and potted mums, cornstalks make an attractive fall display.

Mums are related to dahlias, sunflowers, marigolds, zinnias and cosmos. The relationship is easy to see when you compare the flowers of each. There are 13 identification groups, or classes of mums: Irregular incurve, reflex, regular incurve, decorative, intermediate incurve, pompon, single and semi-double, anemone, spoon, quill, spider, brush and thistle, and unclassified. (For a good graphic of these classes, visit the National Chrysanthemum Society's Web site at:

<http://www.mums.org/journal/articles/classifications_bw.htm>.)

You might wonder if the mums you buy at the big box stores are hardy to our zone. Will they survive through the winter to bloom again next year? I spoke with fellow master gardener Dennis James who owns DJ's Greenhouse in Transfer (1004

Through the Seasons

East Lake Road) about this and he cleared up a little confusion for me. He said hardy mums are not necessarily perennial mums. In other words, "what we call hardy mums are mums that can usually take a light to moderate frost through the fall season," James said. These mums may or may not overwinter in zone 5 gardens.

Garden mums, or perennial mums, are ones you can be sure to see color from year after year, as long as you take care of them once the first killing frosts are past. After die back, mulch your perennial mums with a four to six-inch layer of straw, remove the mulch in spring and cut back dead plant material from the previous season. You can work in a good all-purpose organic fertilizer in early spring and once every two weeks or so through the growing season.

If you're unsure about your box store mums surviving through the winter, why not plant them out in the garden and conduct a little experiment. Mulch one, and not the other; place one close to the house, the other out by the shed or in the middle of one of your flower beds. You might find a micro-climate somewhere that those "average Joe" mums you bought at Wal Mart for $2.99 will find perfect for their new home, come snow or high water!

For a good selection of perennial mums, contact Bluestone Perennials at 1-800-852-5243.

Several years ago while visiting my Mother in Kentucky during fall I noticed some exceptionally gorgeous mums blooming in one of her flower beds. She passed along a clump and I tried them here in my Pennsylvania garden. These were seasonal mums, ones she had picked up at a local box store. They performed well in her garden for years, but didn't do so well here. They tried for a couple of years, with some help from me, I laid down a thick layer of mulch before the onset of winter, snipped the tips and left the main stems with plenty of leaves to help keep them insulated. But without a warmer microclimate for this type of mum, they were doomed for a short life-span from the start. I've since learned that the best home for some pass-along plants is one that closely matches the one where it came from. And the home I made for those mums here in Pennsylvania didn't even come close to the one they had in Kentucky.

Through the Seasons

Individuality

Some people garden through the seasons as if there is only one. Gardeners living in warmer regions of the country may be able to sow and reap ten months out of the year, or they might be year-round gardeners. Folks living in colder regions might even be envious of year-round gardeners. But I for one am not. I like distinctions.

I know it's time to get my seeds ready when the first hints of warm air begin flowing in March. When April's nippy nighttime temperatures are hovering in the 30s and 40s, I know the soil hasn't had a chance to warm up enough to support the roots of tomatoes. By the time the warmer air currents of June, July, and August are ushering in summer's heat, my garden is lush and green, and colorful and weedy.

September and October bring the chilly winds and cold temperatures that signal Jack Frost's arrival. Nature's reds, golds, yellows and reds of autumn trigger an awareness that tells me God is in control, not me or you. December, January, February and March can be snowy months, and the white that blankets the landscape hides and insulates plants that need an extended period of cold - plants that begin a new life in spring.

These four seasons: Winter, spring, summer, and fall, are the passing of one year, one year out of the many thousands that man has tilled the earth and harvested its bounty. For those of us who prefer to see distinctions, there's nothing better than the

Through the Seasons

individuality of winter, spring, summer, and fall as we garden

through the seasons.

Through the Seasons

Seasonal Gardening Tips

Winter

✓ Keep all de-icing and snow melting chemicals sealed and stored in their own separate container.

✓ A home weather station that includes a minimum/maximum thermometer, a rain gauge and a weather log is a good gift for a gardener.

Through the Seasons

✓ Start reviewing and expanding your garden notes to help with next year's plans.

✓ Collect remaining crop residues or other organic matter and add to the compost heap.

✓ Before you attach the snow blade, change the oil in your mower. That way, you won't have to take it back off to do so.

✓ There may still be time to put in spring bulbs, but not much time. If you do, plant them a little deeper than normal.

✓ Cut back overly long canes on your hybrid tea rose so they're not whipping around in the winter winds. Mulch lower canes and crown with straw.

✓ Although the shortest month may seem like one of the longest, don't let February foil your plans for thinking spring. Try germinating plants from fruit seeds; oranges, grapefruits, lemons, tangerines and pomegranates are all good candidates. Put them in warm, moist soil and check for germination within six weeks.

✓ Heavy snow accumulations on shrubs can cause branches to flop and possibly even break off. Gently brush snow from them and consider tying branches together loosely with twine so that the interior is exposed.

✓ Use non-salt de-icing products on your driveways and sidewalks. Sand, kitty litter, and ashes from the wood stove are three alternatives.

Through the Seasons

✓ Keep the feeders full. Winter's chill is still in the air and our feathered friends appreciate the free meal.

✓ If you use a cold frame, check it accordingly as warm spells occur during winter. Open vents as needed.

Spring

✓ If the snow has melted it's a good time to weed, weed, and weed! But keep a wary eye out for those new plants you put in last year.

✓ Once danger of frost has passed, remove winter mulch from roses, hydrangeas, clematis, azaleas and other tender shrubs.

✓ Before the landscape is full and green, take a look at its emptiness and plan a spot for a new hardscape feature such as a birdbath, garden bench or sundial.

✓ In the raised beds, sow seeds of carrots, greens, beets and other root vegetables.

✓ When weather permits, get out and carefully rake debris from around emerging early season perennials such as crocus and irises. They'll appreciate your efforts.

✓ If you think you might have soil problems, or just want to know exactly what's in your garden dirt, consider having it tested now before planting. Stop by your local extension office and pick up a soil test kit. The cost is minimal for what you get in return.

Through the Seasons

✓ Keep a garden journal. Writing down your failures and successes from last year will help you this year.

✓ Still haven't got those mower blades sharpened? Beat the rush and have them sharpened now. Consider buying a new blade. Mulching blades are now available to fit most machines.

✓ Take some time now to get gardening tools and equipment ready for the beginning of the growing season.

✓ If, you've not received your seed order yet, be sure to contact the company you ordered from and have them check the status of your order.

✓ Read up on a few of the bad bugs you might encounter this growing season (Japanese beetles, aphids, etc.). The more you know about garden pests, the more you'll be able to deal with them appropriately, before things get out of hand.

✓ Spring flowering trees and shrubs will soon be showing you what they're made of. Take a close look at other landscapes on the way to and from work when these plants are flowering. You just might find a jewel you'll want to grow yourself.

✓ Don't become an elitist and ignore old archaic things to use in the garden that you might find at yard sales. An idea of what to look for: old re-bar that you can bend and shape into hardscape features; old buckets to use as planters; old wooden-handled shovels, rakes, or hoes for use as posts for hanging pots.

✓ Evergreens in containers dry out faster than ground-planted shrubs, water container-grown conifers more frequently. My moisture test: put your index finger into the soil to the second joint, if no dirt sticks to your finger when you remove it, it's time to water.

✓ If you're trying to maintain a specific look, trim your evergreen regularly, removing stray sprouts as necessary. Stop pruning six weeks before first frost.

✓ Dwarf conifers in containers grow more slowly than standard types and require less pruning. However, even dwarfs eventually outgrow pots and require replacements.

Summer

✓ Mint is ubiquitous, cut a handful, rinse well, and add to cold water for a nice cool minty drink while you're resting in the shade.

✓ Switch to mowing every other week; your grass will look better, your mower will last longer, you'll save gas and decrease harmful emissions.

✓ Most new mowers have mulching blades installed which means you don't have to rake! As an added bonus, grass clippings will decompose adding nitrogen back into the soil.

✓ Weeds are much easier to pull after a good rain, and doing so when it's actually raining can be refreshing and fun.

- ✓ If birds are done eating seeds from purple coneflowers and black-eyed Susans, stems can be cut back to the ground.
- ✓ How are your houseplants on the back porch? Hose them down to wash off dust if rainfall isn't available to do the job.
- ✓ To avoid transplant stress, plant on a cloudy day or in the evening and shade new plants for a day or two if they are in a sunny site.
- ✓ I've noticed a few Japanese beetles on my viburnum. I'm not sure if this will be their preferred food source this year, but I am sure the ones I found on it won't survive in the jar of soapy water I knocked them into.
- ✓ Are your hosta undulatas looking dried and tired? Cut them back and they'll produce new foliage that will last till first frost. (Undulatas are a common variegated variety.)

Fall

- ✓ A fantastically fragrant frilly flower for late spring, 'Angélique' tulips open in June and are blush-pink growing to 18 inches, plant in large groups.

Through the Seasons

- ✓ Deer resistant bulbs for spring include alliums, crocus, grape hyacinth, and daffodil.

- ✓ Looking for a new shrub for the landscape? Viburnums are a good choice. There are many varieties to choose from that should match your needs. 'Aurora' is fragrant with large snowball flowers that turn red to white.

- ✓ Remember those beautiful fall leaves you used to collect as a kid? Revert back to those days for an hour or two and have some fun collecting a few for a garden scrapbook.

- ✓ Don't let fall garden clean up chores overwhelm you. Just do a little at a time, and if you haven't started a compost pile yet, now would be a good time.

- ✓ Cooler temperatures in autumn often leave grasses wet with dew until well after sunrise. Wait until grass dries completely before mowing. Once you notice a slower growth rate, you can probably go ahead and winterize the mower.

- ✓ Be sure to check the garden for any hand tools you might have left lying around. I found a pair of hand pruners this past spring that overwintered.

- ✓ Store your seeds in an airtight plastic container and label it. I'm not into promoting name brand stuff, but for seed storage Tupperware is tops.

- ✓ We always have a couple of amaryllis potted up inside. Now is the time to get yours ready if you want to enjoy them for the year-end holidays.

Through the Seasons

✓   I dug up my cannas last weekend, one chore I'm glad to have out of the way. After drying, pack your canna and dahlia bulbs in sphagnum peat,
vermiculite, or sand. Store in a garage or basement where winter temperatures are between 40-50 degrees.

✓   See all those leaves? Use them, don't burn them, they're instant mulch, they'll decompose over the winter and add valuable nutrients.

✓   Grow 'Aspen,' 'Big Tom,' or 'Ghost Rider' standard orange large pumpkins for fall display.

✓   Wait until the stem is completely dry and brown before harvesting your gourds and pumpkins, leave about four to six inches of stem when cutting.

✓   Create a "bulb sandwich" by layering early bloomers such as May-blooming daffodils eight inches deep at the bottom, on top of them plant April and May-blooming tulips 3 to 5 inches deep, and top it off with March-blooming crocus planted 5 inches deep.

Why I Don't Cook

This isn't an excuse; at least I hope it doesn't sound like one. It is a great big THANK YOU! to my wife, Maureen, for never asking me to cook. Yes, I feel guilty at times for not taking it upon myself to prepare a meal or two, but the way I figure, it all evens out when you consider that I've never asked her to sharpen the mower blades or use the weed eater.

I cooked a meal for Maureen before we married – fried chicken, mashed potatoes, green beans, and a simple salad. For a bachelor, three items on the menu is a pretty good meal. I didn't have much in the way of place settings at the time, and the table cloth was actually a sheet of wrapping paper left over from Christmas that a friend gave me. I don't remember if she ate everything or not, or if she frowned in-between bites, but I do remember feeling quite proud of myself and thinking that I had somehow managed to impress her.

Over the years, 20 of them, she has never stopped impressing me with her cooking skills. I can think of only one incident where something didn't turn out quite like she had planned (I think it was an overcooked pot of soup). That's impressive if you think about how many meals were cooked before and after.

Some might think the yard work vs. chef work comparison isn't quite legitimate, that may be so but I said in the beginning that this isn't an excuse. It's an honorary tribute to the greatest cook I know, who just happens to be my wife and my best friend. I asked Maureen for a few of her favorite fresh garden veggie recipes, she provided what follows.

Mo's Fresh Salsa / Salad

The use of fresh produce is always preferable, but sometimes it's not always immediately available.

Quantities: your preference!

Ingredients:

Chopped tomatoes

Chopped green peppers

Chopped onion

A few cloves of chopped garlic

Chopped hot peppers – jalapeño or Hungarian – just a little or to taste.

Chopped parsley and cilantro (personally, I think cilantro tastes like soap, but what do I know, I don't cook!)

Lime juice – a few squeezes

Mix ingredients together, add salt and pepper to taste. Serve with tortilla chips – fresh and delicious!

For salad, chop ingredients, except for the hot peppers, to a larger dice – ¾ inch or so, but keep hot peppers small. Make as above but add a can of corn and a can of black beans, rinsed. Add balsamic vinegar, olive oil, cumin and chili powder to top off this great salad!

Mo's Bruschetta

Ingredients:

Chopped tomatoes

Chopped garlic, a few cloves

Chopped basil

1 small onion, chopped

1 small green pepper, chopped

1 loaf French bread

Shredded mozzarella and parmesan cheese

Mix ingredients with a little olive oil, balsamic vinegar and salt and pepper. Slice bread to desired thickness and toast, then top with vegetable mixture using a slotted spoon. Sprinkle with mozzarella and parmesan cheese. Bake at 400° for a few minutes or until cheese melts. (Good stuff!)

Through the Seasons

Through the Seasons

Glossary

Advent Wreath: A Christian tradition that uses an evergreen wreath to symbolize the passing of the four weeks of Advent in the liturgical calendar of the Western church. It's usually placed horizontally on a table with four candles.

Annual: A plant or flower that usually gives up the ghost after one growing season.

Aromatic: Having an odor, unpleasant or not.

Amendment: Fertilizer, compost or other natural ingredient added to soil for the purpose of increasing its health.

Black Gold: The healthiest and cleanest type of soil (or dirt) known to man (and the Beverly Hillbillies). See also **humus.**

Bulb: An undeveloped plant packaged in a fleshy storage structure (usually perennials).

Botany: The scientific stuff about plants that hortheads like to talk about.

Bluegrass: (1) A popular cool season lawn grass grown in the northeast. (2) A popular cool all-season genre of folk music usually incorporating acoustic instruments such as the banjo, mandolin, guitar and upright bass.

Carl Linnaeus: An ancient horthead who came up with the coolest method of naming and classifying plants, so cool that his system has been in use for almost 300 years.

Through the Seasons

Container: Pot, planter, or any such object used for displaying plants.

Corm: A glob of mainly stem tissue, except for a few papery scalelike leaves covering the outside. Roots sprout from the bottom and the corm grows into a gladiola or crocus (two types of many flowering corms).

Cosmos: (1) An annual flower in the Aster family of plants that is so easy to grow it almost doesn't need soil. (2) An orderly or harmonious system that incorporates plenty of cosmos.

Dirt: See **soil**.

Dormant: Inactive, restful. Most perennial plants need an extended period of inactivity in order to rejuvenate their energy supplies for the following season. (Most gardeners go dormant during winter.)

Dudes for Palin: A male conservative feminist movement during the presidential election of 2008. Millions of men showed their support for VP candidate Sarah Palin by wearing "Proud to be voting for a hot chick" buttons.

Entomologist: A know-it-all specializing in insects.

Garden: (1) (noun) A plot of ground where flowers, vegetables, herbs or fruits are grown. (2) (verb) To work in a garden. (3) (adjective) Relating to or used in a garden.

Gardenologist: A know-it-all specializing in gardening.

Greenhouse: A special glass building designed to house plants 365 days a year. Temperature, humidity, and other environmental conditions within the greenhouse are controlled by gardenologists.

Hardy: A term used to indicate whether or not a plant is cold tolerant to a specific gardening zone. For example, zinnias are not hardy in zone 5 and cannot overwinter. (Some gardeners don't overwinter very well either.)

Heaving: A soil condition common to the northeast, caused by thawing and refreezing of ground during winter. (Plant roots become exposed.)

Heirloom: (1) A plant variety that is open-pollinated known for superior taste and/or unusual coloration. (2) A valued possession passed down from generation to generation.

Hollow: A small valley between mountains. Alternate pronunciation: **holler** (southern colloquialism).

Horthead: (Hort-head) Horticultural know-it-all (may or may not be a master gardener or gardenologist).

Humus: See **Black Gold**.

Jonquil: Daffodil, or narcissus flower. Also called jonquil in the south, some species are known for their ability to naturalize.

Locavore: Someone who recognizes the importance of: 1) Purchasing locally grown produce. 2) Backyard vegetable gardening. 3) Environmental awareness and sustainable gardening with little or no chemical pesticides/insecticides/herbicides.

Through the Seasons

Microclimate: That area of ground just below your drier vent, the first couple of feet out from the base of your house extending along the sunny side and protected from weather extremes, or any such area where the climate differs from the surrounding area.

NPK: Nitrogen, **P**hosphorous, and **P**otash (Potassium), are the NPK ratings on lawn and plant fertilizers. Nitrogen helps plants keep strong foliage, phosphorous aids root and flower growth and development, and potassium is important for overall plant health.

Overwinter: Spend the winter. Some diseases and insect larvae and pupae have the capability to spend winters (stay alive) snuggled under thick mulch or unfinished compost, reappearing in early spring to wreak havoc.

Pawpaw: Kentucky banana (fruit of the native North American Pawpaw tree).

Pollinate/Cross Pollinate: Pollinate – the transfer of pollen resulting in fertilization and sexual reproduction. Cross pollinate – pollen delivered to a flower from a different plant, sometimes done intentionally in order to create new varieties.

Rhizome: Plants with horizontal stems that grow near or slightly above the soil line. Calla lilies, cannas, and bearded iris are three examples.

Runoff: Water that flows over the ground surface, especially during heavy rains. This condition is a concern because certain chemicals used in the lawn and garden/agricultural industries

Through the Seasons

could possibly be carried into fresh water lakes, streams, rivers and possibly seep into underground aquifers.

Solstice: Twice yearly the tilt of the Earth is just so that its axis is pointed toward or away from the sun. This incident causes the sun to reach its northernmost or southernmost greatest distance from Earth.

Soil: See **dirt.**

Tuber: A specialized plant structure; a white or Irish potato is a stem tuber, a dahlia is root tuber.

Twitter: 1) A social networking service that uses what's known as tweets. Tweets are text-based messages no longer than 140 characters. 2) Bird talk. (Avian tweets are unlimited.)

Yankee Dime: An insincere kiss

Epilogue

(It's not something I had planned on putting in but I think it sounds neat when you say it – epilogue – pretty too.) This little endnote will give you my contact information should you decide, or feel the need to get in touch with me. I'm quite visible on the web. My website is thewritegardener.com; it's nothing fancy, just a place I use to post a gardening article now and then. I'm also blogging at thewritegardener.wordpress.com. I don't update my blog as much as others but try to post at least once a week, I'm liable to write about anything there. Find me on Facebook here: www.facebook.com/thewritegardener, and on Twitter too: http://twitter.com/WriteGardener.

And then there's always the old fashioned thing called pen and paper if you dare write a letter: TC Conner, 1604 Mercer Grove City Road, Mercer, PA 16137 is the address. I don't use those old tools anymore, but it's said that history repeats itself, so if you write me, I promise to write you back.

Thanks for reading my book, God bless!

Through the Seasons